THE EATING AND

C000140388

"...an opinionated little compendium.
~ New York Times

"...irresistible little guide."
~ Chicago Tribune

"an elegant, small guide..."
~ Minneapolis Star Tribune

"Makes dining easy and enjoyable."
~ Toronto Sun

""...a terrific primer for first-time visitors."
~ Houston Chronicle

*""...opening up the world of good eating with their
innovative paperback series."*
~ Salt Lake Tribune

"It's written as if a friend were talking to you."
~ Celebrity Chef Tyler Florence

"...travelers who know their cervelle *(brains) from*
cervelle de canut *(herbed cheese spread)."*
~ USA Today

"Order like an Italian."
~ Boston Globe

•

ABOUT THE AUTHOR

Andy Herbach is the author of the *Eating & Drinking* series of menu translators and restaurant guides, including *Eating & Drinking in Paris*, *Eating & Drinking in Italy*, *Eating & Drinking in Spain and Portugal* and *Eating & Drinking in Latin America*.

Andy is also the author of several books published by Europe Made Easy Travel Guides, including *Paris Walks*, *Europe Made Easy*, *Italy Made Easy*, *Paris Made Easy*, *Berlin Made Easy*, *Amsterdam Made Easy*, *French Riviera Made Easy*, *Provence Made Easy*, *Oslo Made Easy*, and *Barcelona Made Easy*.

You can e-mail comments, additions and corrections to eatndrink@aol.com.

UPDATES

Updates to this guide can be found at www.eatndrink.com.

ACKNOWLEDGMENTS

Marian Olson (our Miss Know-It-All English editor) and Angelina Bellotti (our Italian editor) were of great help in the original edition of this book.

Special thanks to those who have helped us find the restaurants in this guide, especially Mark Berry and Dan Schmidt who suffered through many meals and countless bottles of wine on our behalf.

Cover photo by Christopher Michel from wikimedia. Back cover photo from pixabay.com.

Andy thanks Karl Raaum for all his help.

Books in this series are available in bulk purchases at special discounts for promotions or premiums. Special editions, including corporate imprints and personalized covers, can be created in large quantities. For more information, contact the publisher or authors.

EATING AND DRINKING IN

Venice

Andy Herbach

EUROPE MADE EASY TRAVEL GUIDES

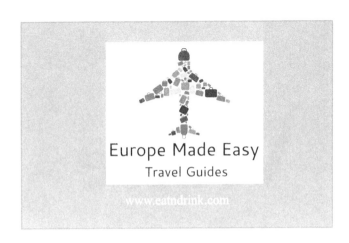

Europe Made Easy
Travel Guides
www.eatndrink.com

Illustrations: Michael Dillon

ISBN: 9781072930389

Introduction

Can you imagine a foreign traveler who speaks basic English understanding what prime rib is? Or a porterhouse? Veggie platter, anyone? Buffalo wings? Sloppy joes?

Even people who speak passable Italian can have trouble reading a menu. You may know *ricotta* cheese, but not *malfatti di ricotta* which means "badly made," a reference to the handmade dumpling with *ricotta* cheese filling. You may be surprised to find *puttanesca* (which means *in the style of a prostitute*) on the menu. It's a sauce of tomatoes, capers, anchovies, black olives and garlic.

Understanding the customs and food of a country helps travelers understand the people who live in the country.

If you love to travel as we do, you know the importance of a good guide. The same is true of dining. A good guide can make all the difference between a memorable evening and a dizzyingly bad one. This guide will help you find your way around a menu written in Italian. It gives you the freedom to enter places you might never have before and order a dinner without shouting, pointing and hand waving. Instead of fumbling with a bulky, conspicuous tourist guide (most of which usually include a very incomplete listing of foods) in a restaurant, this book is a pocket-sized alphabetical listing of food and drink commonly found on menus in Italy.

Although, now that we think about it, a dinner without shouting and hand waving is not truly Italian.

Of course, traveling to a foreign country means something differ-ent to everyone. For every vacation there are different expecta-tions, different needs, and every traveler has his or her own idea of what will make that vacation memorable. For us, the making of a memorable vacation begins and ends with food.

We spent the morning staring at the Sistine Chapel and the Vatican Museum, but what stands out in our minds is the wonderful lunch in the *trattoria* afterward. The creamy shrimp pasta dish was as heav-enly as Michelangelo's masterpiece. We spent a morning driving to see the Leaning Tower of Pisa, but the grilled lamb in Lerici made the day.

We know the panic of opening a menu without recognizing one word on it and the disappointment of being served something other than what you thought you'd ordered. On our first trip to Europe, we were served a plate of cold brains; we thought we had ordered chicken. This guide was created for the traveler who wants to enjoy, appreciate and experience authentic cuisine *and* know what he or she is eating.

The next time you find yourself seated in a red-tiled courtyard with the scent of simmering garlic in the night air and an incomprehensible menu in your hands, simply pull this guide from your pocket and get ready to enjoy the delicious cuisine of Italy.

In Italy and Ticino (the Italian-speaking region of Switzerland), the menu is almost always posted outside of the restaurant or in a window. This makes choosing a restaurant easy and fun as you "window shop" for your next meal.

Remember that the dish that you ordered may not be exactly as described in this guide. Every chef is (and should be) innovative. What we have listed for you in this guide is the most common version of a dish.

If a menu has an English translation it does not mean that the translation is correct.

In Italy, it's customary to order a first course (pasta, rice or soup), a second course (meat, poultry or fish) and a side dish (salad, potato or vegetable). Rarely does an Italian order only a first course (such as ordering only pasta), but that doesn't mean you can't.

Tipping

A service charge is almost always added to your bill (*il conto*) in Italy. Depending on the service, it's sometimes appropriate to leave up to 5%. Most locals round up to the next euro and it's okay if that is what you do, too. Travelers from the U.S. sometimes have trouble *not* tipping. Remember, you do *not* have to tip. The menu will usually note that service is included (*servizio incluso* or *servizio compreso*).

You will often find *coperto* or cover charge on your menu (a charge just for placing your butt at the table). This flat fee is usually between one euro to three euros per person.

Mealtimes

In northern Italy, lunch is served from noon to around 2 p.m., and dinner from 7 p.m. to 10 p.m. In the south, lunch is served from 1 p.m. and dinner from 8 p.m. No "early bird special" in Italy. Ticino's hours are the same as in northern Italy.

Europeans joke that you can tell a U.S. tourist from his fanny pack, clothes and ubiquitous bottle of mineral water. Tap water is safe in Italy and Switzerland. Occasionally, you will find *non potabile* signs in rest rooms (especially in the rest stops of highways). This means that the water is not safe for drinking.

Waiters and waitresses will often bring *acqua minerale* (mineral water) to your table. You will be charged for it, so if you do not want mineral water ask for *acqua semplice* or *acqua di rubinetto* (tap water).

Restaurants in This Guide

Each of our recommended restaurants offers something different. Some have great food and little ambiance. Others have great ambiance and adequate food. Still others have both. Our goal is to find restaurants that are moderately priced and enjoyable. All restaurants have been tried and tested. Not enough can be said for a friendly welcome and great service. No matter how fabulous the meal, the experience will always be better when the staff treats you as if they actually want you there rather than simply tolerating your presence.

Times can change and restaurants can close, so do a walk-by earlier in the day or the day before, if possible. Our full list of restaurants starting on page 99 includes many of the eating establishments listed below.

Types of Eating Establishments

Bacaro: Venetian wine bar serving snacks like Spanish *tapas.*
Bar: Bars serve espresso, cappuccino, rolls, small sandwiches, alcoholic beverages and soft drinks.
Bottiglieria: Simple drinking establishments with limited menus but plenty of bottles of wine. Originally, these "bottle shops" served only liquor. Also called *fiaschetteria*, *cantina* or *trani*.
Enoteca: Wine bar.
Gelateria: Shop serving *gelato* (ice cream).
Grotta: Ticino has many *grotti*. These are village restaurants that take their name from caves used to store food and wine. Originally, a *grotto* was a simple eating establishment, but today many are quite expensive with extensive menus.
Locanda: Found in the country, serves regional meats and seafood.

Osteria: A tavern or wine shop. This name has also come to refer to a restaurant. These can also be called *cucina* or *hostaria*.
Paninoteca: Usually serves only sandwiches.
Pasticceria: Pastry shop.
Pizza Rustica: Common in central Italy; serves large rectangular pizzas with thicker crusts and more toppings than usually found in a *pizzeria*. You can order as much as you want, and pay by weight.
Pizzeria: We think you can figure this one out.
Ristorante: A restaurant.
Rosticceria: A deli, sometimes with a few tables, where you can order grilled meats (especially chicken).
Tavola Calda: Small restaurant with take-out or fast foods and usually with a few tables.
Trattoria: Less expensive family-run restaurant, usually not too fancy.

Tips for Budget Dining in Italy

There is no need to spend a lot of money in Italy to eat good food. There are all kinds of fabulous foods to be had inexpensively all over Italy.

Eat at a neighborhood restaurant or *trattoria*. You'll always know the price of a meal before entering, as almost all restaurants in Italy post the menu and prices in the window. Never order anything whose price is not known in advance. For instance, if you see *etto* on a menu in Venice this means that you're paying by weight (an *etto* is 100 grams), which can be extremely expensive.
Delis and food stores can provide cheap and wonderful meals. Buy cheese, bread, wine and other snacks and have a picnic. Remember to pack a corkscrew and eating utensils when you leave home.

Lunch, even at the most expensive restaurants listed in this guide, always has a lower price. So, have lunch as your main meal.

Restaurants that have menus written in English (especially those near tourist attractions) are almost always more expensive than neighborhood restaurants.

Street vendors generally sell inexpensive and good food. For the cost of a cup of coffee or a drink, you can linger at a café and watch the world pass you by for as long as you want. It's one of Italy's greatest bargains.

And don't eat at McDonald's, for God's sake.

Speaking Italian - Pronunciation Guide

If you're looking for a comprehensive guide to speaking Italian, this is not the the place. These are simply a few tips for speaking Italian followed by a very brief pronunciation guide. It's always good to learn a few polite terms so that you can excuse yourself when you've stepped on the foot of an elderly lady or spilled your drink down the back of the gentleman in front of you. It's also just common courtesy to greet the people you meet in your hotel, and in shops and restaurants, in their own language.

In Italian, you pronounce every letter. E and i are soft vowels when used with consonants. The final e is always pronounced.

The second to the last syllable is stressed. If there is an accent in the word, stress the accented syllable.

a like in father.
au like ow in cow.
b the same as in English.
c **ca, co** and **cu** like k in keep.
– **ce** and **ci**, like ch in cheap.
ch like k in kite.
d the same as in English.
e like in day.
ei like ay in lay.
f the same as in English.
g **ga, go** and **gu** like g in gate.
– **ge** and **gi** like j in jar.
gh like g in goat.
gl like gl in glow except before i, then like lli in million.
gn like ni in onion.
h silent. H after a consonant gives it a hard sound.
i like ee in jeep.
ie, io, iu, **i** is pronounced as y (ie. *pensione* ~ pen syo neh).
k/l/m/n the same as in English.
o usually like o in boat.
p/q the same as in English.

ue, ui, uo, the u is pronounced like a w (ie. *buono* ~ bwo no).
r with a slight trill.
s like s in sit except between two vowels, then like s in hose.
sc **sca, sco** or **scu** as sk in skirt.
– **sce** or **sci** as sh in sharp.
t the same as English.
u like oo in foot.
v the same as in English.
z the same as ds in fads.

Pronunciation
_____

CA – KA
CE – CHAY
CI – CHEE
CHI – KEY
CHE – KAY

Confused?

ITALY

ABRUZZO & MOLISE
(Off-the-Beaten-Track Italy)

Along the Adriatic coast are
the mountainous regions of
Abruzzo and Molise. The
quiet hill towns are in great
contrast to the Adriatic resorts.
The most notable tourist venue
is the Abruzzo National Park, a
place for hikers and nature lovers.
Outside this nature reserve is Scanno,
a popular summer resort town. L`Aquila
(which means "the eagle") is the capital of Abruzzo and is a business center.
Few tourists from the United States and
Canada visit this part of Italy. If you're
looking for off-the-beaten-track destinations and mountain scenery, Molise and
Abruzzo will certainly please.

Inland, you will find menus dominated
by *capretto* (baby goat), *agnello arrosto* (roast lamb), and
porchetta (roast pig). On the coast (in restaurants not serving tourist fare) try *brodetto* (fish soup). *Centerbe* (a green herb liquor)
accompanies many meals. For dessert, try *confetti* (flower-
shaped candy made from sugar-coated almonds).

APULIA (The "Heel" of Italy)

Apulia (Puglia) is the "heel" of Italy. Oppressively hot in July
and August, a rainy day is rare. Apulia is a large wine-producing
region. The area is not frequented by many North American tourists. The baroque town of Martina Franca and the whitewashed
town of Locorotondo are in the wine region and worth a visit. Part
of the coast is heavily industrialized with immense steelworks.

Bari is a modern port and a common departure point for travelers to Greece. *Trulli*, dome-shaped whitewashed stone buildings, are indigienous to the area. The largest collection of *trulli* can be found near Alberobello. The Adriatic fishing ports have architecture similar to the old Venetian ports. Taranto is a modern town, as is the important port of Brindisi, another frequent departure point for visits to Greece. Not to be missed is the lovely Baroque town of Lecce.

Focaccia barese (stuffed pizza), often with *burrata* (very buttery cheese), *triglia* (red mullet), *spigola* (sea bass), *orecchiette con le cime di rapa* (ear-shaped pasta with turnips) and *tiella di riso e cozze* (a mussels, rice and potato dish) can all be found on Apulia's menus. Some avoid the *polpi arricciati* ("curled octopus") when they see that the octopus is beaten and twirled in a basket in order to get the desired "curled" shape. *Bianco di Martina* is a common fortified wine found in Apulia.

BASILICATA
(Undiscovered Italy)

This area was once known as Lucania. One of Italy's smallest regions, Basilicata is also its poorest. Mountainous and barren, Basilicata is not visited by many tourists. The capital city of Potenza was badly damaged in a 1980's earth-quake. The hill town of Maratea is dramatically situated on the coast. Here, in small villages such as Metaponto and Matera, you experience the simple Italy.

Spicy *sugna piccante* (pork sauce) flavors many dishes. *Maiale* (pork) is found on most menus, and cured meats like the sausage *luganega*, *luganica* or *lucanica* (there are even more spellings than this!) are common. *Peperoncini* (small hot green peppers preserved in oil) are added to many dishes. Try *scamorza* cheese (the local version of aged *mozzarella*).

CALABRIA (The "Toe" of Italy)

Sun, white-sand beaches, rugged mountains, olive groves and the huge rock of Scilla are all found on the "toe" of Italy. The area was once known as Magna Graecia, and there are villages where a Greek dialect is still spoken. The mountain towns such as Serra San Bruno remain as they were several hundred years ago. Rossano is a beautiful medieval town overlooking a great ravine. Consenza is a town built on a steep hillside with an interesting (almost dilapidated) look to it. Many tourists find themselves in modern Reggio on their way to Sicily. The small towns of Pizzo and Tropea are worth a visit to experience the true Calabria. We would be remiss if we did not mention that some areas of Calabria are strongholds of the local mafia and not recommended for travel.

Costolette d'agnello (lamb chops) and *pesce spada* (swordfish) are found on most menus. *Novellame* is a spread of salted anchovies and *peperoncino* sauce. Pasta is often served with chickpeas (*ceci*). *Stracotto* is a beef stew which in Calabria includes carrots, mushrooms, onions, nutmeg and cloves. *Caviale del sud* or "caviar of the south" is a dish of fried fish preserved in oil and powdered with *peperoncino*. *Fichi* (figs) are featured in many desserts.

CAMPANIA (Naples, Capri & the Amalfi Coast)

Naples, in the shadow of Vesuvius, is congested, noisy, has a reputation as dangerous, and is not an easy city for the tourist. After a quick view of Naples' old town along the harbor, most head for the nearby ruins of Herculaneum and Pompeii. It's an eerie experience walking through nearly perfectly preserved ancient communities buried by the volcanic eruption of Vesuvius. The volcanic island of Ischia and nearby Capri are

often overrun
by day trippers
in high season.
Although it can
be expensive,
Capri (with its
breathtaking

vistas) remains the favorite of many returning visitors. The
gateway to the Amalfi coast is Sorrento, perched over the sea.
The Amalfi coast is the most spectacular coastal drive in Italy
(if you have the nerve to drive it in high season). Positano has
a great beach with a view of the town perched on the bluff.
Amalfi and Ravello, further down the Amalfi coast, have
spectacular views. The Amalfi coast reigns as one of the most
scenic and photographed coasts in the world.

Seafood is prevalent along the coast, especially *polpi affogati*
(octopus in a spicy tomato sauce). Pizza, said to have originated
in Naples, is found in many varieties. *Pizza alla Napoletana* is
pizza with tomato sauce and anchovies. You will eat tomatoes
here like you have never had before. Many pasta dishes are
served *al pomodoro* (with a tomato sauce). Meat is often cooked
alla pizzaiola (in a tomato sauce with garlic). *Partenopea* on a
menu simply means served Naples style. For dessert try *sfoglia-
tella* (flaky pastry filled with sweet *ricotta* cheese).

EMILIA-ROMAGNA (From the Adriatic Sea to Central Italy)

The Romans built a grand road from Rimini on the Adriatic Sea
to Piacenza in central Italy. The towns that now make up this
region developed along this road, the Via Emilia. Piacenza is a
major industrial city with a lovely downtown. Parma (which lends
its name to the famous Parma ham or *prosciutto*), Modena (home
to the Ferrari and Maserati automobiles), Bologna (a learning
center, important city for commerce, and *the* food town in Italy),
and Ferrara (less spoiled by modern times than the others) are all
towns with important historic centers. Imposing Ravenna is in
contrast to the most popular Adriatic resort of Rimini. Be careful,

15

as Rimini can be quite dull, even completely closed, off
season and extremely overcrowded in season.

The coast features *brodetto* (fish soup). *Prosciutto di Parma* (Parma
ham) is common as is *risotto* (the famous Italian rice dish). Suckling
pig is called *lattonzolo* here. For dessert, try *castagnole* (chestnut
fritters). True Italian food is rare in Rimini, which has revised its
menus to cater to the European package tourist.

FRIULI-VENEZIA GIULIA (Trieste & the Austrian Border)

This region borders on Austria and Slovenia. Udine is the capital
but Trieste draws the most attention. Trieste, which remained under
United Nations control until 1954, is an interesting mix of Austrian
and Italian with a Slavic influence from the former Yugoslav repub-
lics. The architecture along the port demonstrates the mix of rulers
in Trieste. Our several trips to Trieste have made us realize that this
area is often, unfortunately, overlooked by tourists. White wine is
produced in the hills of Friuli-Venezia Giulia. Visit the towns of
Colli Orientali and Collio. The small mountain towns along the
Austrian border allow the visitor to experience a mixture of Italy
and Austria.

Jota is a minestrone found here and usually contains sauerkraut.
Polenta (cornmeal mush) is found everywhere. *Brodetto* (fish
soup) is common in the coastal area of this region. *Cialzons* is a
sweet-and-sour pasta dish found here. The town of San Daniele is
the home of *prosciutto di San Daniele* (a cured ham). The Slavic
influence is found in the Trieste dessert of *gubana* (sweet bread
roll) and the Austrian influence is found in the many coffeehouses
of Trieste.

LAZIO (Rome & its Environs)

Lazio (also called Latium) is the region around Rome. To try to list
Rome's main attractions would require another guide. Rome can
be a frustrating city (it can be hard to carry on a conversation while
walking down the street due to the constant traffic noise). But, dif-

ficulties aside, few places
in the world have so many
important sites in such
a small area, including
the Vatican with its
Sistine Chapel, Circus
Maximus, the Spanish
Steps, the Trevi Fountain, the catacombs...

Sperlonga, San Felice Circeo, Santa Severa and Santa Marinella
are all coastal towns worth a visit. Ostia is a large coastal city
near Rome and was the main Roman port. Its impressive ruins are
an easy day trip from Rome. In inland Lazio, you may visit Tivoli
(with Hadrian's Villa), Palestrina, the mountain town of Subiaco
and the walled town of Viterbo.

Rome is said to have 5,000 restaurants where you can eat just
about anything. After a grueling day of sightseeing, stop in a
small restaurant (*trattoria*), drink some wine and eat a hearty dish
of pasta such as one served *all' arrabbiata* (in a spicy tomato and
herb sauce) or *alla carbonara* (with bacon, cheese, olive oil and
eggs). Meals often start with *bruschetta* (garlic toast) and end
with *grappa* (of which we drank a little too much on our first
night here). When in Rome...

LE MARCHE (The Apennines Mountain Region)

The Apennines Mountains separate Le Marche from the rest of
Central Italy. Ancona, on the Adriatic coast (a common departure point for Venice) is a modern port town. Pilgrims visit the
house of the Virgin Mary in Loreto (brought here, according
to legend, by angels). Urbino, one of the lesser-known great
Renaissance cities, looks much as it did in the fifteenth century.
In the Tronto River Valley, scenic Ascoli Piceno is another Le
Marche town worth visiting. Most travelers head for the crowded (package tour-filled) coastal towns. These crowded resorts
are in great contrast to the sedate hill towns.

Truffles (*tartufi*) are a specialty here, and summer peaches (*pesche*) and plums (*susine*) are some of the best fruits you will ever taste. *Vincigrassi* (baked lasagna dish), *olive all'ascolana* (large stuffed olives), *porchetta* (roast suckling pig) and rabbit (*coniglio*) are popular. *Brodetto di pesce* (fish soup) is found along the coast. In Ancona, *brodetto* contains thirteen varieties of fish.

LIGURIA (The Italian Riviera)

Wedged between mountains and the sea, the coastal region of Liguria stretches from the French border to Tuscany and is a popular tourist destination. Genoa, a large industrial city, is also Italy's biggest port. Tourists usually visit only the old, central part of the city. West of Genoa toward the French border are the bright tourist towns of Ventimiglia and Bordighera. San Remo (with its famous casino) is the largest resort. East from Genoa, you will find the resort of Nervi with beautiful parks. Further down the coast are the resort towns of Camogli, Rapallo, Santa Margherita and of course, perhaps the best known and most beautiful Italian port of Portofino. One drawback is the gridlock in and out of Portofino in high season. Sestri Levante makes a good base for exploring the highlight of any trip to Liguria, the Cinque Terre, five beautiful towns, which until recently were accessible only by train or a series of hiking paths. Perched on dramatic cliffs above the sea, you will experience car-free serenity and an Italy of old. Down the coast is Lerici (where we had one of our most memorable meals in an open-air restaurant on the port).

Seafood is dominant in Liguria, especially *branzino* (sea bass), *aragosta* (lobster), *vongole* (clams), *zuppa di datteri* (fish soup), *stoccafisso* (dried cod), *ciuppin* (fish and vegetable stew) and *fritto misto di frutti di mare* (mixed seafood, usually grilled).

18

Sadly, seafood is becoming less common because of pollution and overfishing in the Mediterranean. *Basilico* (basil) grown in the hills above the sea forms the basis of *pesto* and is common in the cuisine of Liguria. Try *ravioli di magro* (pasta stuffed with herbs and *ricotta* cheese).

LOMBARDY (Milan & the Lake District)

Fashionable, modern Milan is an important center of Italian commerce. If you like to shop, Milan is the place. Tourists often visit four important sites: the Duomo (cathedral, especially the ornate roof), La Scala (the opera house), the Last Supper (at the church of Santa Maria delle Grazie), and the Galleria Vittorio Emanuele (the famous glass-domed shopping center).

In great contrast to Milan is the Lake District, including Lakes Orta (often, regrettably, ignored), Maggiore, Como, and Garda. The towns that line these lakes remain dotted with former palaces (many now resorts) with impressive formal gardens. Many believe the Lake District is Italy at its best. On Lake Como, Bellagio is the most famous resort, but Varenna, with its tiny harbor and splendid beach, is the favorite of many.

Trota (trout) is popular in the Lake District. Lombardy specialties include *stracotto* (pot roast), *ossobuco* (braised veal shank) and *capretto* (roast kid). You will find many dishes served *alla milanese* (battered with eggs and breadcrumbs and fried). *Risotto alla milanese* is a popular rice dish made golden from the ingredient saffron. *Gorgonzola* (a delicious blue cheese) is often found in pasta dishes. Lombardy cheeses also included *crescenza* (a soft, buttery cheese) and *mascarpone* (a very creamy cheese). *Torrone* (honey-and-almond nougat) is a common dessert.

PIEDMONT & VALLE D'AOSTA (Turin & the Alps)

Sometimes the Alpine regions of Piedmont (which means "foot of the mountain") and Valle d'Aosta (north of Piedmont) feel more like France or Switzerland than Italy. Valle d'Aosta has two official languages: Italian and French. Many come to the largest city in these regions, Turin (Torino), to see the Shroud of Turin (believed by some to be the cloth in which Christ's body was wrapped after the crucifixion). North of Turin, into Valle d'Aosta, is Saint Vincent (a popular gambling resort). Any trip to this area would not be complete without a visit to Breuil-Cervina at the base of the Matterhorn (Monte Cervino) with breathtaking views of this famous mountain peak. Courmayeur, another Alpine resort, is the gateway to Mont Blanc (Monte Bianco) on the French border. The walled city of Aosta is nestled in the Alps. Asti (yes, as in the wine), Novara, Vercelli, and Casale Monferrato are all towns with impressive medieval towers. If you're looking for beautiful mountain scenery, don't miss these regions.

Piemontese on a menu means "Piedmont style" or with white truffles. *Tartufi bianchi* are famous white truffles from Alba and Asti. *Alla Valdostana* on a menu means "Valle d'Aosta style" and usually means with ham and cheese. Roast game, sausages and butter play heavy roles in the local diet. *Tajarin* is thin ribbon pasta made golden with egg yolks. *Fonduta* (fondue) is popular. The French influence can be found in *crespelle* (crêpes). You will find *cervo* (venison), *carbonade* (beef cooked in wine and onions) and *arrosto misto* (grilled meats) here along with *trota* (trout). *Giandujotti* are hazelnut chocolates found in Turin and one of our favorite treats. *Torta di nocciole*, hazelnut cake, is a must.

SAN MARINO (Europe's Oldest Country)

With about only 25,000 people and 24 square miles, San Marino
(totally surrounded by Italy) claims to be Europe's oldest existing
country. San Marino's official name is the Most Serene Republic
of San Marino, and is located 15 miles inland from the Adriatic
Sea resort of Rimini. Its chief industries are tourism and the sale
of postage stamps. Mt. Titano, upon which San Marino sits, must
be climbed after you leave your car. There are three medieval for-
tresses on the mountain. The capital, also named San Marino, is a
maze of attractive narrow streets.

Food is typical Italian. You'll find *coniglio* (rabbit) and *nidi di
rondine* (pasta rolls). Don't miss *caciatella* (San Marino's version
of crème caramel).

SARDINIA (SARDEGNA)

The island of Sardinia is located about 115 miles off the western
coast of Italy in the Mediterranean. Ten miles to the north is
the French island of Corsica. Sardinia has been a part of Italy
since 1861. Cagliari, the capital, is on the south coast, which is
known for its ancient ruins. For the most part, Sardinia remains
unspoiled from its rocky coast to its mountainous interior. The
northeastern Costa Smeralda (Emerald Coast) is the only area
where tourist development has arrived. Those looking for peace
and quiet and even isolation should experience the mountainous
inland region of Barbagia.

Lobster (*aragosta*) is plentiful along the coast, and the northern
coast of Sardinia is sometimes referred to as the lobster coast.
Lamb (*agnello*), rabbit (*cunillu*) and trout (*trota*) are ubiquitous.
Grilled meats are a specialty. The shepherds of Sardinia feast on
pane carasau, which is also known as *carta da musica* (music
paper). Durham wheat, salt, water and yeast are the simple ingredients for this wood fire-baked bread. You will find this thin,
crispy bread used as a pizza crust.

Other specialties of Sardinia include *porceddu* (roast suckling pig which is the "national" dish of Sardinia), *cascà* (couscous), and many honey-based desserts such as *sebadas* (deep-fried cheese-filled ravioli soaked in honey).

SICILY (SICILIA)

F rench, Arabs, Spanish and Italians have all controlled Sicily, the largest and most populated island in the Mediterranean. Travelers will find some of the best-preserved Greek and Roman ruins here, along with the ornate architecture of its churches and palaces. Agrigento is home to the most important archaeological site in Sicily, the Greek "Valley of the Temples." Siracusa (Syracuse) is also known for its Greek and Roman ruins. The capital is Palermo, but most travelers head to the medieval town of Taormina on the east coast in the shadows of Mount Etna, an active volcano. Messina (destroyed by both an earthquake and the bombs of World War II) has bland, modern architecture, and is in strong contrast to the picturesque fishing port of Cefalù.

Sicilian cuisine is not simply pasta and olive oil but incorporates Italian, Greek, French, Spanish and Arab influences. Some specialties are *pasta con le sarde* (pasta with fresh sardines), *pesce spada* (swordfish), and the simple *cicina* (a mixture of fried small fish). Other specialties are *caponata* (sweet-and-sour sauce with eggplant, tomatoes, onions and peppers), *pasta alla Norma* (pasta with a tomato, basil and eggplant sauce topped with *ricotta* cheese) and *costoletta alla siciliana* (thin slices of veal or beef topped with chopped garlic and *parmesan* cheese, then breaded and deep-fried).

Desserts, and Sicilians

are famous for their desserts, include *cannoli* (pastry tubes filled with sweetened *ricotta* cheese) and *cassata alla siciliana* (layered spongecake).

Marsala wine (from the town of the same name) is a fortified wine that can range from rich and sweet to dry.

TICINO (Italian-Speaking Switzerland)

Ticino is the main Italian-speaking canton or region of Switzerland. Palm trees, Italian architecture, Swiss orderliness and Italian food all make Ticino (with its famous resorts of Lugano and Locarno) a great travel destination. Ticino is Switzerland's southernmost canton, bordering on Italy, and has been a part of Switzerland since the early 1800s. This region has always remained strongly Italian. Italian is one of four official languages of Switzerland (along with French, German and Romansh).

Specialties found in Ticino are *risotto ai fiori di zucca* (a rice dish made with a heavy cream base and zucchini flowers stirred in along with *parmesan* cheese), *pancetta arrotolata* (rolled bacon flavored with cloves), *capretto* (baby goat), *fritto misto* (breaded and fried lake fish), *cotto antico* (bay leaf-flavored salami), and *giambonetti di pollo* (stuffed chicken leg). Bread is a staple in all meals, especially bread with a thick crust dusted with flour called *crusca*. Two common cheeses found in Ticino are *formaggini di capra* (fresh goat's-milk cheese) and *formaggini d'Alpe* (a common cow's-milk cheese). Both of these cheeses are eaten with olive oil, salt and pepper.

TRENTINO-ALTO ADIGE (The Dolomites)

The Alto Adige is the far north of Italy and is more like Austria than Italy. The Dolomite Mountains dominate this area. At the Brenner Pass, on the border with Austria, is the town of Bolzano/Bozen (Austrian until 1918). Near Bolzano is the wine town of Caldaro. Bressanone/Brixen is a beautiful mountain town and the Alto Adige's oldest city. Ortisei, San Martino and Madonna di Campiglio are all summer and winter resort towns. Breathtaking views abound in Brunico/Bruneck. Merano has an interesting old town and famous spas. Trento, the capital of Trentino, is more Italian than Austrian and remains an attractive and architecturally interesting town.

Food here is more German than Italian (especially the farther north you travel). Game, dumplings (*knoedel*) and cured ham (*speck*) all stress the German influence. Sauerkraut (*crauti*) is featured heavily in dishes, as are *wurstel* (hot dogs and brats). For dessert, apples, grown in large numbers in the region, are often added to the Germanic dessert of *strudel*.

TUSCANY (One of the World's Most Popular Destinations)

There are so many picturesque towns in Tuscany, space allows only a few highlights. With unspoiled hills, perfectly preserved towns and great food and wine, Tuscany is one of the most popular tourist destinations in Italy and the world. Since child-hood, we wanted to see the Leaning Tower of Pisa (and the nearby and lesser-known baptistery). There's so much more to this vibrant and interesting city than just the tower. Siena's main square, the Piazza del Campo, and ornate cathedral are only two gems in the beautiful town with (thankfully) a car-free cen-ter. San Gimignano, with its walls and towers, is an incredibly picturesque town. The hilltop towns of Lucca, Montepulciano, Montalcino and Pienza are all worth a visit. Of course, Florence is the favorite of many visitors to Italy. Its wealth of art, housed in buildings which themselves are art, leaves many visitors want-ing to return again and again.

Start your meal with *crostini* (toasted bread with various top-pings). *La bistecca alla Fiorentina*, a T-bone steak, must not be missed, nor should any of the *pecorino* cheeses. Menus often include dishes served *alla lepre* (in a rabbit-based sauce), *cinghiale* (wild boar), *arista* (roast, seasoned pork loin), and *ribollita* (bean and/or cabbage soup which means "twice-cooked soup). *Chianti*, *chianti* and more *chianti*. Enough said!

UMBRIA (Assisi & the Hill Towns North of Rome)

Green hills, towns spared from industrialization, and wonderful dining combine to make Umbria an outstanding Italian destination (especially by car). Perugia is Umbria's largest city with a historic city center, but most tourists come here to visit the smaller towns like Gubbio in northern Umbria. Orvieto is located on a monumental square-shaped rock visible for miles. Don't miss this impressive and well-preserved town (or a taste of its famous wines). Assisi is home to a huge basilica built in memory of local hero St. Francis. It's ironic that such a huge basilica was built for such a humble man, or that the streets are filled with shops selling St. Francis keychains. Still, Assisi, perched on a hill, is a memorable sight. Walled Spoleto (home of the well-known art festival) is dominated by a large castle and is surrounded by wooded countryside.

Tartufi (truffles) are a specialty here, especially the black truffle (*tartufo nero*). *Stringozzi* (homemade pasta) is used in many dishes, especially in Spoleto. *Strozzapreti* (dumplings with meat sauce) is a dish with the strange name of "priest stranglers" after a priest allegedly choked on it. *Palombacci* are small songbirds cooked whole on a spit. For dessert, try *stinchetti* (marzipan cakes). Of course, no one thinks of eating in Umbria without drinking one of the many fine wines of this region.

VENETO (Venice & its Environs)

Veneto is the region around Venice. Despite the tourists, the sometimes smelly canals and the often inflated prices, Venice is unlike anywhere else in the world. Many cities claim to be pedestrian only, but Venice is truly car-free. Don't just take a day trip here. Once the day trippers leave, Venice becomes a quiet, romantic maze of streets with spec- tacular architecture. As many times as we have visited, we are always amazed at the splendid beauty of Venice with its buildings rising out of the sea. Don't miss the Piazza San Marco, the Bridge of Sighs, the Basilica di San Marco and the Doge's Palace. If time permits, visit the islands of Murano (famous for its ornate glass), Burano (famous for its lace), San Michele (Venice's island cem- etery) and Torcello (for a taste of an almost deserted island).

Veneto includes the cities of Vicenza, Padua (where you can see the "uncorrupted" tongue of St. Anthony), Verona and Treviso. Many towns remain unspoiled and rarely visited by tourists, including Valpolicella (home of this popular Italian red wine), the hills of Colli Euganei (home of hot thermal springs), and Asolo. North of Treviso are the mountain resorts of Cortina d' Ampezzo and Belluno.

Cape sante (scallops), *baccalà* (dried cod), *fegato alla veneziana* (liver with onions), *seppie* (cuttlefish), and *gran- seola* (crab) are all specialties of Venice. *Polenta* (the famous cornmeal mush) is found throughout the region. *Carpaccio* is thinly sliced raw beef served in a sauce, and was named by the owner of Harry's Bar in Venice after a famous Venetian painter. *Prosecco* is a slightly sparkling wine from Veneto and worth a try. While in Venice, don't miss having an evening drink or *caffè* in the Piazza San Marco.

26

This is a brief listing of some familiar English food and food-related words that you may need in a restaurant, followed by a list of phrases that may come in handy.

anchovy, acciuga (acciughe)
appetizer, antipasto (i)
apple, mela (e)
artichoke, carciofo (i)
ashtray, portacenere
asparagus, asparago (i)
bacon, pancetta
baked, al forno
banana, banana (e)
bean, fagiolo (i)
beef, manzo (di bue)
beefsteak, bistecca (di manzo)
beer, birra (e)
beverage, bevanda (e)
bill, conto (i)
bitter, amaro (a)
boiled, bollito/lesso
bottle, bottiglia
bowl, scodella
bread, pane
bread rolls, panino (i)
breakfast, prima colazione
broiled, graticola/griglia
broth, brodo
butter, burro
cabbage, cavolo (i)
cake, torta (e)
candle, candela
carrot, carota (e)
cereal, cereale (i)
chair, sedia

[handwritten notes in margin:]
Words that end in A or O are singular
Words that end in E or I are plural
bottiglia ~ bow-tee-Lee-ah
Words and letters in parentheses indicate plurals.
cereale ~ cheer-ee-ah-Lay

check, conto (i)
cheers, salute/cin cin
cheese, formaggio (formaggi)
cherry, ciliegia (e)
chicken soup, brodo di pollo/zuppa di pollo
chicken, pollo
chop, costoletta (e)
clam, vongola (e)
cocktail, cocktail
cod, baccalà/merluzzo
coffee, caffè (also black coffee)
coffee w/hot water
   (to dilute), caffè amercano
coffee w/milk, caffè latte
coffee (decaf), caffè hag/caffè decaffeinato
coffee w/cream, caffè con panna
cold, freddo (a)
corn, mais
cover charge, pane coperto
cucumber, cetriolo (i)
cup, coppa
   tazza coffee/tea cup
custard, crema
dessert, dolce (i)
dinner, cena
dish (plate), piatto
drink, bevanda (e)
dry (as in wine), secco
duck, anitra/anatra
egg, uovo (a)
espresso, caffè espresso
fish, pesce
fish soup, zuppa di pesce
fork, forchetta
french fries, patate fritte
fresh, fresco (a)
fried, fritto (a)/fritti (e)

caffè italiano.   *caffè americano.*

freddo ~ FRAY-doh

dolce ~ dole-chay

cena ~ chain-ah

forchetta.

forchetta~ FOR-KAY-TAH

fruit, frutta
game, cacciagione/selvaggina
garlic, aglio
gin, gin
glass, bicchiere
grapefruit, pompelmo
grape, uva
green bean, fagiolino (i)
grilled, griglia or alla griglia
half, mezzo (a)
ham (cooked), prosciutto cotto
ham (cured), prosciutto crudo
hamburger, hamburger
honey, miele
hors d'oeuvre, antipasto
hot, caldo (a)
iced, ghiacciato
ice coffee, caffè freddo
ice cream, gelato (i)
ice (on the rocks), ghiaccio or con ghiaccio
ice water, acqua fredda
iced tea, tè freddo
ketchup, ketchup/salsa di pomodoro
knife, coltello
lamb, abbacchio/agnello
large, grande
lemon, limone (i)
lettuce, lattuga
little (a little), un pó
liver, fegato (fegatini)
lobster, aragosta (e)
loin, lombata
lunch, pranzo
marinated, marinato (a)
match, fiammifero (i)
meat, carne
medium (cooked), a puntino or normale

Bicchiere.
BEE·KEE·AY·RAY

griglia
GREE-LEE·AH

ghiacciato ~
ghee-AH·chee-A·Toe

coltello.

melon, melone
menu, carta or menù
milk, latte
mineral water, acqua minerale
mineral water (sparkling), acqua minerale gasata
mineral water (w/out carbonation), acqua
   minerale non gasata
mixed, mista (o)
mushroom, fungo (i)
mussel, cozza (e)
mustard, senape
napkin, tovagliolo
noodles, taglierini/pasta
octopus, polipo/polpo
oil, olio
olive oil, olio d'oliva
omelette, frittata
on the rocks (w/ ice), con ghiaccio
onion, cipolla (e)
orange, arancia (arance)
orange juice, succo d'arancia
overdone, ben cotto
oyster, ostrica (ostriche)
pastries, dolci/paste
peach, pesca (pesche)
pear, pera (e)
pea, pisello (i)
pepper (black), pepe
pepper (bell), peperone (i)
perch, pesce persico
pineapple, ananas
plate (dish), piatto
please, per piacere
plum, susina (e)
poached, affogato
pork, maiale

Tovagliolo ~
Toe·vah·Lee·oh·Lo

funghi.

cipolla ~
chee·polla

per piacere ~
pare·pee·ah·chair·AY

maiale ~
my·AL·LAY

potato, patata (e)
poultry, pollame
prawn, gamberetto (i)
rabbit, coniglio
rare, al sangue
raspberry, lampone (i)
receipt, ricevuta/scontrino
rice, riso
roast, arrosto
salad, insalata
salt, sale
sandwich, sandwich/panino (i)
sauce, salsa
saucer, piattino/sottocoppa
sautéed, saltato (i)/saltata (e)
scallops, cappe sante
scrambled, strapazzate
seafood, frutti di mare
seasoning, condimento (i)
shrimp, scampo (i),
    gamberetto (i)
small, piccolo (i)/piccola (e)
smoked, affumicata (o)
snail, lumaca (lumache)
sole, sogliola (e)
soup, zuppa (e)/minestra (e)
spaghetti, spaghetti
sparkling wine, spumante
specialty, specialità
spinach, spinaci
spoon, cucchiaio
squid, calamaro (i)
steak, bistecca
steamed, a vapore
stewed, in umido
strawberry, fragola (e)
sugar, zucchero

Coniglio
Co-NEE-LEO

ricevuta~
ree-chay-voo-tah

gamberetto.

Lumaca.

cucchiaio~
KOO KEE AYE OH

Zucchero~
ZOO-KARE-OH

sugar substitute, dolcificante

supper, cena

sweet, dolce *dolce—DOL-CHAY*

table, tavolo

tea, tè

tea w/lemon, tè al limone *TAZZA*

tea w/milk, tè al latte *di*

teaspoon, cucchiaino *tè.*

thank you, grazie

tip, mancia

toasted, tostato

tomato, pomodoro (i)

trout, trota

tumbler (glass), bicchiere *tacchino*

tuna, tonno *TA-KEE-NO*

turkey, tacchino

utensil, posata (e)/utensile (i)

veal, vitello

veal scallop, scaloppa di vitello

vegetable, legume (i). *Verdura (e)* green vegetables

vegetarian, vegetariana (o)

venison, carne di cervo

vinegar, aceto

waiter, cameriere

waitress, cameriera

water, acqua *Unless there's a*

well done, ben cotto *written translation,*

whipped cream, panna montata *it pretty much*

sounds like it

wine, vino *Looks, only more*

wine (full-bodied), vino corposo *Italian sounding.*

wine list, lista dei vini *DON't forget*

wine (red), vino rosso *to pronounce that*

wine (rosé), vino rosé *final 'E'!*

wine (white), vino bianco

Helpful Phrases

Prego (*preh-go*) can mean: thank you, you're welcome, this way (with a hand gesture), please, okay, and can I help you.
Ciao means hello *and* goodbye. *chow*
Italians answer the phone with ***Pronto?*** *prohn-toh*

please, per favore *pehr-fah-voh-ray*

thank you, grazie *graht-see-ay*

yes, sì *see*

no, no *noh*

good morning, buon giorno *bwohn-jor-noh*

good afternoon/evening, buona sera *bwohn-ah- say-rah*

good night, buona notte *bwohn-ah-noht-tay*

goodbye, arrivederci *ah-ree-veh-**dehr**-chee*

do you speak English?, parla inglese? *par-lah een-gleh-zay*

I don't speak Italian, non parlo l'italiano *nohn par-loh lee-tah-lee-**ah**-noh*

excuse me, mi scusi (or *scusi*) *mee-skoo-zee*

I don't understand, non capisco *nohn kah-pees-koh*

waiter, cameriere *kah-meh-ree-eh-ray*

waitress, cameriera *kah-meh-ree-eh-rah*

I'd like..., Vorrei... *voh-reh-ee*

I'd like a table, Vorrei un tavolo *voh-reh-ee oon-tah-voh-loh*

I'd like to make a reservation, Vorrei prenotare *voh-reh-ee preh-noh-**tah**-ray*

for one person, per uno (una)   *OONO*
DOO AY
for two, per due (2), tre (3), quattro (4), cinque (5),   *TRAY*
sei (6), sette (7), otto (8), nove (9), dieci (10)   *KWATRO*
CHINK·WAY
today/tomorrow, oggi *oh-jee*/domani *doh-mah-nee*   *SAY*
SET·TAY
by the window, vicino alla finestra *vee-chee-noh*   *OH TOE*
*ah-lah fee-**neh**-strah*   *NO VAY*
dee AY CHI
outside, fuori *fwoh-ree*/**inside,** dentro *dehn-troh*

where is?, dov'è *doh-vey*

the bathroom, il bagno/la toilette *eel bahn-nyoh lah twah-leh-tay*

the bill, il conto *eel kohn-toh*

service (not) included, servizio (non) incluso *sehr-veet-see-oh (nohn) een-kloo-zoh*

33

a mistake, errore *eh-roh-ray*

credit card, carta di credito *kar-tah dee kreh-dee-toh*

how much does this cost?, quanto costa? *kwahn-toh koh-stah*

what is this?, cos' è questo? *koh-zeh kweh-stoh*

I did not order this, Io questo non l'ho ordinato *ee-oh kweh-stoh nohn loh or-dee-nah-toh*

this is, questo è *kweh-stoh eh*

a little, un po' *oon poh*

hot, caldo (a) *kahl-doh*/**cold,** freddo (a) *freh-doh*

spicy (hot), piccante *pee-kahn-tay*

vegetarian, vegetariano/a *veh-jeh-tah-ryah-noh ah*

I don't eat,... Non mangio *nohn mahn-joh*

allergic, allergico (a) *ah-lehr-jee-koh*

dairy, latticini *lah-tee-chee-nee*

wheat/gluten, frumento *froo-mehn-toh*/glutine *gloo-tee-nay*

seafood, frutti di mare *froo-tee dee mah-ray*

shellfish, molluschi e crostacei *moh-loo-skee ay kroh-stah-cheh-ee*

nuts, noci e altra frutta secca *noh-chee ay ahl-trah froo-tah seh-kah*

peanuts, arachidi *ah-rah-kee-dee*

diabetic, diabete *dee-ah-beh-tay*

kosher, kasher *kah-shehr*

no caffeine, senza caffeina *sehn-sah kah-feh-ee-nah*

no alcohol, niente alcool *nee-ehn-tay ahl-kohl*

vegetarian, vegetariano (a) *veh-jeh-tah-ree-ah-noh*

vegan, vegano (a) *veh-gah-noh*

undercooked, troppo crudo *troh-poh kroo-doh*

overcooked, troppo cotto *troh-poh koh-toh*

delicious, delizioso (a) *deh-lee-tsee-oh-zoh*

light (low-fat), leggero *leh-jeh-roh*

open, aperto *ah-pehr-toh*/**closed,** chiuso *kee-oo-zoh*

Monday, lunedì *loo-nay-dee*

Tuesday, martedì *mar-tay-dee*

Wednesday, mercoledì *mehr-cohl-ay-dee*

Thursday, giovedì *joh-vay-dee*

Friday, venerdì *vay-nehr-dee*

Saturday, sabato *sah-bah-toh*

Sunday, domenica *doh-mehn-nee-kah*

abbacchio, lamb
abbacchio alla cacciatora, pieces of lamb braised w/rosemary, garlic, wine & peppers
abbacchio alla romana, pieces of lamb cooked until brown, then roasted in a rosemary, garlic, vinegar & anchovy sauce
abbacchio brodettato, pieces of lamb cooked in a broth of lemon, parsley & beaten eggs
abboccato, a medium-sweet wine
abbrustolito, toasted
abruzzese, red pepper sauce
acciuga (acciughe), anchovy
acciughe al limone, anchovies w/lemon-based sauce
acerbo, sour
aceto, vinegar
aceto balsamico, balsamic vinegar. Aged vinegar used in many dishes, especially salads
acetosella, sorrel
acido, sour
acini di pepe, pasta for soup in the shape of peppercorns
acqua, water
acqua brillante, tonic water
acquacotta, bread & vegetable soup
acquadella, small whitebait fish
acqua di rubinetto, tap water
acqua di seltz, seltzer water/soda water
acqua fredda, ice water
acqua gasata, carbonated water
acqua ghiacciata, ice water
acqua minerale, mineral water
acqua minerale frizzante, extremely carbonated water
acqua minerale naturale, mineral water w/out carbonation
acqua naturale, tap water
acqua non gasata, water w/out carbonation
acqua non potabile, do not drink the water!
acqua pazza, sauce of tomato, garlic, oil, parsley & chili pepper
acqua semplice, tap water
acqua tonica, tonic water
Acquavite, brandy/distilled spirit flavored w/caraway
affettato, sliced

acciuga ~
AH·CHEE·oo·ga

*"Acqua cotta"
means
cooked water*

35

affettato (i), cold cut

affogato, poached. This can also refer to ice cream soaked in coffee or liqueur

affumicato, smoked

agliata/all'aglio, garlic sauce

aglio, garlic

aglio e olio, w/garlic & olive oil

aglione, mixture of garlic, sea salt, rosemary & sage

agnello, lamb

Aglio.

agnello alla turca, lamb stew w/raisins

agnello con salsa di uovo, lamb w/egg sauce.

agnolotti, filled pasta (square shaped)

agone, freshwater fish found in the lake country (the size of sardines)

agresto, juice of unripened grapes

agro, lemon juice & olive oil dressing

agrodolce, sweet & sour sauce

ai/al/all'/alla, in the style of/with

ajula, sea bream

ala, wing

alaccia, large sardine

alalunga, albacore (a type of tuna)

Albana, dry to semi-sweet wine from Emilia-Romagna

albicocca (albicocche), apricot

albume, egg white

alcolica, alcoholic. *Una bevanda alcolica* is an alcoholic beverage

alcool, alcol

Aleatico, dessert wine (made from muscat grapes)

alette, wing

alfabetini, alphabet noodles for soup

al forno, baked

alfredo, w/butter & cream sauce

al fresco, outside (in the fresh air)

alice (i), anchovy

allodola (e), lark

alloro, bay leaf

ALLORO.

amabile, slightly sweet wine

amarena (e), sour cherry

amaretti, macaroons

amaretto, sweet almond-flavored liqueur

amaro, bitter/bitter cordial (bitters)

amatriciana, bacon, tomato & spices sauce

Agresto is sometimes used in place of vinegar

amburghese/amburgo, hamburger/ground meat
amburghese alla tirolese, hamburger served w/onion rings
Americano, Campari, vermouth & lemon peel
ammiru, prawns in Sicily
analcolico (i), non-alcoholic
ananas, pineapple
anatra, duck
anatroccolo, duckling
anelli/anellini, small circular
    pasta for soup (ring pasta)
aneto, dill
anguidda, another name for eel in Sicily
anguilla (e), eel
anguilla alla veneziana, eel braised
    w/tuna & lemon sauce
anguria, watermelon
anice, anise
animelle, sweetbreads
animelle alla salvia, sweetbreads w/sage
anisetta, anise-flavored liquor
anitra, duck
anitra germano, mallard duck
anitra selvatica, wild duck
annegati, slices of meat in wine
antipasto (i), appetizer
antipasto alla marinara/antipasto di mare/antipasto di
    pesce, assorted seafood
antipasto misto, assorted appetizers
aperitivo, aperitif
arachide (i), peanut
aragosta (e), lobster (crayfish)
arancia (e), orange. *All' arancia* means w/orange juice
aranciata, orangeade/orange soda
arancino (i) di riso, breaded ball of cooked rice stuffed w/meat
& deep-fried. It gets its name from its resemblance to an
orange
argentina, argentine fish
arigusta, crawfish
aringa, herring
aringa affumicata, smoked herring
arista, roast, seasoned pork loin
arista alla fiorentina, roasted pork rubbed w/garlic paste,
    cloves, salt, rosemary, pepper

In Perugia Anguilla can also refer to an eel shaped pastry created originally by nuns.

arista di maiale/arista di suino, pork loin
arrabbiata, all', w/a spicy tomato & herb sauce
arrostetti, small roast
arrosti misti freddi, a selection of cold roasted meats
arrostini, veal chops
arrostino, small roast
arrostino annegato, small veal roast
   served with mushrooms
arrostite, grilled/roasted
arrosto/arrostito, roast/roasted
arrosto alla genovese, a roast w/onions, mushrooms
   & tomatoes
arrosto alla montanara, pot roast
arrosto con pastine, roast w/dough crust
arrosto di manzo, roast beef
arrosto in porchetta, roast suckling pig stuffed w/garlic,
   bacon & herbs
arrosto misto, mixed roast meats
arrosto morto, pot roast
arsella (e), mussel
asciutta (o), dry. Also refers to pasta w/sauce
   (as opposed to pasta for soup)
asiago, sharp cheese (round-shaped cheese)
asiago dolce, mild *asiago*
asparago (i), asparagus
asparago alla bismark, asparagus w/melted butter & fried egg
asparago alla milanese/asparago all'uovo, asapagus topped
   w/melted butter, *parmesan* cheese & fried egg
assortito (i), assorted
astaco/astice, lobster
Asti Spumante, sparkling white wine
attorta, fruit- & almond-filled pastry
Aurum, orange liqueur
avvoltino, standing roast or rolled roast
babà, spongecake covered w/rum
babaluci, snails in tomato & onion sauce
bacca (e), berry
baccalà, salt cod
baccalà alla fiorentina, salt cod floured & fried in oil
   & tomato sauce
baccalà alla lucana, salt cod cooked w/peppers
baccalà alla vicentina, salt cod w/onion, parsley, garlic,
   anchovies & cinnamon

bacio, chocolate hazelnut (means "kiss")

bagna cauda/bagna caoda, hot vegetable dip w/anchovies

bagnet, sauce (in Piedmont)

balsamella, bechamel/white sauce

banana (e), banana   *Good Guess!*

bar, serves espresso, cappuccino, rolls, small sandwiches, alcoholic beverages and soft drinks

barbabietola (e), beet

Barbaresco, soft red wine from Piedmont (lighter & drier than *Barolo*)

Barbera, dry red wine   *Andy hates*

barbe rosse, beets   *beets even*

Bardolino, pale, light red wine   *in Italy.*

Barolo, rich red wine from Piedmont

basilico, basil

bastoncini, bread sticks (means "little sticks")

battuta scanello, pounded round steak

battutina al prosciutto, hamburger mixed w/cured ham

battuto, finely chopped herbs, onions, celery & carrots

battuto di manzo, ground beef

bavette (i), thin, flat pasta

beccaccia, woodcock

beccaccino, snipe (game)

beccafico, warbler/song bird

belga, Belgian endive

bellini, *Prosecco* & peach juice. Try one at Harry's Bar in Venice   *"Bel Paese"*

bel paese, smooth, mild & soft cheese   *means*

ben cotto, well done   *beautiful*

bensone, lemon cake   *country*

besciamella, white cream sauce

bevanda (e), drink/beverage

bevanda compresa, cost of drinks included

bianchetti, small anchovy (or sardine)

bianchi, white

bianco, white wine

Bianco di Martina, a fortified wine found in Apulia

bianco, in, w/butter (w/out a sauce)

bibita (e), drink/beverage

bibite analcoliche, soft drinks

bicchiere, glass   *Bicchiere.*

biete, Swiss chard   *BEE·KEE·AY·RAY*

bietole, beet/Swiss chard

bietole alla padella, Swiss chard cooked w/butter &/or oil
bietoline, beet greens
bietolini, Swiss chard
bignè/bignole (con crema), cream puff
bigoli, larger form of spaghetti
biova/biovetta, round bread loaf
birra, beer
birra alla spina, tap beer
birra analcolica, no-alcohol beer
birra bionda, light beer
birra chiara, light beer (lager)
birra di barile, draft beer
birra importata, imported beer
birra in bottiglia, bottled beer
birra in lattina, beer in a can
birra scura, dark beer
biscotto (i), cookie/biscuit/cracker/spongecake
biscotti di prato, cookies w/pieces of almond
biscuit tortoni, dessert of beaten egg whites & macaroon
  crumbs topped w/whipped cream & toasted almonds
bismark, alla, usually means served w/a fried egg
bistecca, steak
bistecca alla bismark, fried steak w/an egg on top
bistecca alla fiorentina, T-bone steak
bistecca alla pizzaiola, steak w/tomato & garlic sauce
bistecca di manzo, beef steak
bistecca di vitello, veal scallop
bistecca Fiorentina, T-bone steak
bistecca impanata, cutlet/chop
bistecche, steaks
bistecchine, thin steaks
bitto, firm, smoked cheese
bobe, sea bream
boccolotti, short tubular pasta
bocconcini, diced veal w/tomato
  & white wine sauce/*mozzarella* balls
boldro, monkfish in Tuscany
boletus, porcini mushrooms
bollito (i), boiled. Can also mean meat or fish stew
bollito di gallina, boiled chicken
bollito di manzo, boiled beef
bollito misto, mixed boiled meats
bolognese, alla, usually means a tomato & meat sauce

BiRRA

*Bistecca
Impanata
is often breaded
and fried
in butter*

"*bocconcini*"
*means
mouthful*

bomba di riso, rice dish w/ground meat & herb fillings

bombette, pork shoulder stuffed with melted cheese.
A specialty in Apulia

bombolone (i), doughnut

bonèt, chocolate cream dessert. A specialty in Piedmont

borlotti, type of bean

boscaiola, means "woodsman style" & can refer to many
things, including w/wild mushrooms

bosega, mullet

botolo, mullet

bottarga, fish eggs (tuna roe that has been salted & pressed)

bottiglia, bottle

bove, beef

bovoletti/bovoloni, small snails in Venice

brace, alla, on charcoal

braciola (e), rib steak/chop/cutlet

braciola di maiale, pork chop

bracioletta, small slice of meat

bracioletta a scottadito, lamb chops (charcoal grilled)

bracioline/braciolone, meat roll

braciolone alla napoletana, breaded steak, rolled & stewed

branzino, bass. *Branzinotti* is small sea bass

brasato, braised/braised meat w/wine

bresaola, thinly sliced cured raw beef

briciole di pane, breadcrumbs

brioche, buns/rolls/small loaf (used for breakfast)

broccoletti, broccoli

broccoletti di rape, turnip greens

broccoletti strascinati, broccoli sautéed w/garlic & bacon

broccolo (i), broccoli

brodetto, rich fish soup

brodo, broth/soup/bouillon.
In brodo means cooked in broth

brodo di manzo, consomme/beef broth

brodo di pollo, chicken soup

brogue, sea bream

brovada, marinated turnips w/pork sausage

Brunello, full-bodied red wine from Montalcino

bruschetta, grilled bread w/garlic & olive oil (frequently
topped w/tomatoes &/or onions)

brut, very dry wine

brutti, small almond cakes

bucaniera, tomato & garlic seafood sauce

41

bucatini, hollow spaghetti noodles

bucatoni, same as *bucatini*, but larger

budino, custard/pudding

budino alla toscana, cream cheese w/raisins, almonds, sugar & egg yolks

bue, beef

burrata, a very buttery cheese found in Apulia

burrida, fish stew or casserole. In Sardinia this refers to a poached & marinated fish dish

burrini, a type of hard, aged cheese

burro, butter

burro maggiordomo, butter w/lemon juice & parsley

alla cacciatora means in the style of the hunter

busecca, tripe & vegetable soup

buttiri, a type of hard, aged cheese

cacao, cocoa

cacasor cioccolata, cocoa

cacciagione, game

cacciatora, alla/cacciatore, w/mushrooms, wine, tomatoes & herbs

cacciucco, spicy fish soup

cachi, persimmons

caciatella, a crème caramel dessert

cacio, *pecorino* cheese

caciocavallo, a hard, aged cheese made of whole milk

cacio e pepe, sauce made of black pepper & *pecorino* cheese

cacio e uova, w/cheese & egg

caciotta, mild cheese

caciucco, fish soup

Traditionally there must be as many types of fish in the soup as C's in caciucco.

caffè, coffee

caffè al vetro, coffee served in a glass

caffè americano, American-style coffee (Italian coffee diluted w/hot water)

caffè con panna, coffee w/cream

caffè corretto, *espresso* w/a shot of liquor (usually brandy)

caffè doppio, coffee (a double serving)

caffè espresso, *espresso*

caffè freddo, iced coffee

caffè hag, decaffeinated coffee

caffè latte, coffee w/steamed milk

caffè lungo, coffee w/water (weaker coffee)

caffè macchiato, coffee w/a small amount of warm milk
caffè nero, black coffee
caffè ristretto, small, thick & strong
    coffee (stronger than an *espresso*)
calamaretto (i), small squid
calamari, squid
calamari fritti, fried squid
calamito, grey mullet
caldo (a)/caldi (e), warm or hot
caldaro, fish & potato soup
calzone (i), folded & stuffed pizza
cameriera, waitress
cameriere, waiter
camicia, in, poached
camomilla, camomile tea
camoscio, small deer (chamois)
campagnola, alla, w/vegetables & herbs
Campari, red aperitif w/a bitter, quinine taste
campo, del, wild. *Cicoria del campo* is wild chicory
candita (o), candied
canederli, dumplings made w/ham, sausage & breadcrumbs
canestrelli, sweet pastry/small sea snail or scallop
cannella, cinnamon
cannellini, small white beans found in Tuscany
cannelloni, large tube pasta stuffed w/fillings
cannelloni al forno, stuffed & browned in oven
cannelloni alla Barbaroux, stuffed w/ham, veal & cheese
cannelloni alla laziale, stuffed w/meat & onions
cannelloni alla napoletana, stuffed w/ham & cheese
    w/tomato & herb sauce
cannelloni alla piemontese, stuffed w/veal, ham & cheese
cannocchie, see *canoce*
cannoli alla siciliana, *ricotta* cheese-filled pastry
    w/sugar glaze
cannolicchio, razor-shell clam
cannolo (i), custard-filled pastry w/candied fruit or sweet
    white cheese (*ricotta*). This
    also refers to a short pasta tube
canoce, Venetian word for
    cannocchie which is neither a
    shrimp nor a lobster but some-
    thing in between
cantarello, chanterelle mushroom

caffè

Cantarello.

cantucci, almond biscuits
capelli d'angelo, thin noodle soup ("angel hair")
capellini, long, thin, fine spaghetti
capelunghe, razor clams
cape sante, scallops in Venice
capitone, large eel
capocollo, smoked pork salami
caponata, cold dish of eggplant & vegetables.
Eggplant, celery & onions are fried separately &
cooked in a sweet & sour sauce of raisins, tomatoes,
pine nuts, sugar & vinegar
caponata di melanzane, eggplant & pepper stew
cappelle di funghi, mushroom caps
cappelletti, rings of pasta filled w/ground meat.
Some think they look like little caps
cappello da prete, a triangular
sausage ("priest's hat")
cappero (i), caper
cappesante, scallops (means
"sacred shells")
capponcello ruspante al forno,
roast farm-raised capon
cappone, capon
cappon magro, vegetables & fish stacked high on a plate
cappuccino, coffee w/steamed milk
capra, goat
caprese, *mozzarella* & tomatoes. **Pasta caprese** is pasta
w/tomatoes, *mozzarella* & basil. *Caprese* means
from the island of Capri
capretto, baby goat
capretto al forno, roasted kid stuffed w/herbs
capretto alla pasqualina, roasted baby goat (an Easter dish)
capricciosa (o), chef's special (means "caprice" or "whim")
caprino, mild goat's-milk cheese
caprino fresco, a fresh goat's-milk cheese
caprino romano, hard goat's-milk cheese
capriolo, small deer (roebuck)
caraffa, carafe
caramellate, caramelized
caramella (e), candy (not chocolate)
caramello, caramel
carbonade, beef cooked in wine & onions
carbonara, pasta w/bacon (or ham), cheese, olive oil & eggs

44

carbonata, grilled pork chop. Sometimes this
refers to beef stew in red wine

carciofi alla giudea, deep-fried artichokes
(prepared in the shape of a rose).
This term means "Jewish-style artichokes"

carciofi alla romana, artichokes stuffed w/garlic, parsley &
mint, cooked in olive oil & white wine

carciofi in pinzimonio, raw artichokes in an oil dressing

carciofini in umido, artichole hearts sautéed in garlic & tomatoes

carciofini sott'olio, artichokes in olive oil

carciofino (i), small artichoke

carciofo (i), artichoke. The bottoms of artichokes are the *fondi di carciofi*

cardo (i), cardoon, a vegetable that looks like celery
but tastes like artichokes

carne, meat

carne a carrargiu, spit-roasted meat

carne cruda all`albese, slices of raw steak

carne di cervo, venison

carne macinata, ground meat

carne per arrosto in pentola, pot roast

carne tritata, ground meat

carone, large white beans

carota (e), carrot

carpa/carpione, carp

carpaccio, thinly sliced raw beef w/sauce. Named by the owner
of Harry's Bar in Venice after a famous Venetian painter

carpaccio di branzino, slices of raw sea bass w/a sauce

carpione, in, served cold w/vinegar sauce

carrargiu, spit-roasted

carré, sliced bread ("square")

carrè di..., roast loin of... *Carrè di agnello* is rack of lamb

carrello, al, served from the food cart

carrettiera, tuna, garlic & pork sauce

carruba, carob

carta, menu

carta da musica, flat, crispy bread of Sardinia. See *pane carasau*

carteddate/cartellate, fried pastry dipped in honey

cartoccio, al, roasted (often in a paper bag, foil or other
covering). The covering is opened at the table

carvi (grani di), caraway (seeds)

casa, house. *Della casa* means "house specialty"

casalinga (o), homemade

cascà, the Sardinian version of couscous

casoncelli, pasta stuffed w/ground meat

cassata, ice cream (or sweet *ricotta* cheese) w/candied fruit

cassata alla siciliana, *ricotta* cheese-filled layered cake
  w/sugar glaze

cassata gelata, various flavors of ice cream w/candied fruit

casserola/casseruola, casserole

cassoela/cassoeula, pork casserole

castagna (e), chestnut

castagnaccio, chestnut cake

castagnole, chestnut fritters

castellana, stuffed veal cutlet

Castelli Romani, white table wine
  from the area southeast of Rome

castrato, mutton

catalogna, a type of salad green (like spinach, often cooked)

cauladda, Sardinian soup of cabbage, beans, sausage & meats

cavalla, mackerel. Also refers to a female horse

cavatappi, tubular pasta in the shape of a corkscrew

cavatelli/cavatieddi, homemade pasta

caviale, caviar

caviale del sud, "caviar of the south." Calabrian dish of dried
  small fish preserved in oil & powdered w/*peperoncino*

cavoletti, Brussels sprouts

cavolfiore, cauliflower

cavolini di Bruxelles/cavoli di Brusselle, Brussels sprouts

cavolo (i), cabbage

cavolo broccoluto, broccoli

cavolo riccio, kale

cavolo rosso, red cabbage

cavolo verde, green cabbage

cazzoeula, pork casserole

cecatelli, homemade pasta

cece (i), chickpea/garbanzo

ceche, baby eels

ceci alla Pisana, chickpea stew

cedrata/cedro, a large fruit that resembles a lemon.
  The peel is used for flavoring

cee alla Pisana, baby-eel dish from Pisa

cefalo, grey mullet

cena, dinner

Cavoletti

EELS BREED in fresh water & mature in the sea.

cena — chain·ah

cenci, fried pastry

Centerbe, green herb liqueur

cèpes, porcini mushroom

Cerasella, cherry liqueur

cereale, cereal

cerfoglio, chervil

cernia, grouper

Certosino, green or yellow herb liqueur.
This is also the name for a soft & mild cheese

cervella, brains

cervo, venison

cestino di frutta, a basket of fruit

cetriolino (i), pickle

cetriolo (i), cucumber

cevapcici, grilled meatballs found near Italian/Slovenian border

charlotte, spongecake & whipped-cream dessert

Chianti, well-known medium-bodied red wine from Tuscany.
Chianti Classico comes from the center of the Chianti
region, is aged for at least one year & is more complex.
Riserva denotes a *Chianti* aged for at least two years

chiare, egg whites

Chiaretto, young & popular rosé wine

chicche, small potato *gnocchi*

chifferi, "c"-shaped tubular pasta

chiocciola (e), snail/sea shell-shaped pasta

chiocciolina, little snail

chiocciolini, spiral-shaped buns

chiodi di garofani, cloves

chiodino (i) a type of mushroom

chiodo di garofano, clove

ciabatta, large, coarse bread loaf

ciauscolo, soft, fatty pork sausage

cialda (e), waffle/wafer

cialledda, vegetable soup w/bread, olives, tomato, hard-boiled
eggs & olive oil. A specialty in Basilicata

cialsons/chialzons, sweet & sour pasta

ciambella/chiambella/ciambelline, donut (not fried like North
American donuts)

cibo, food

cibreo, chicken-liver dish

cicale di mare, type of shrimp (this crustacean is found off the
coast of Italy. The name means "grasshopper")

47

cicchetti/cicheti, snacks served in Venice. Similar to *tapas*

cicina, mixture of small fried fish

cicoria, chicory/endive

ciliegia (e), cherry

cima, stuffed veal served cold

cima alla genovese, veal stuffed w/mushrooms & sausage

cimalino, *cima* served w/beans. ***Cimalino di manzo*** is stuffed breast of beef

cime di rape, turnip greens

cinese, Chinese

cinghiale, wild boar

Cinque Terre, a dry, light white wine from the spectacularly beautiful five towns on the western coast of Italy

cioccolata, chocolate

cioccolata calda, hot chocolate

cioccolato, chocolate (hot chocolate)

ciociara, a seasoned meat sauce

cioppino, fish stew (this word is usually used only in the United States)

cipolla (e), onion

cipollina (e), chive

cipolline novelle, green onions

cipollotti, spring onions

ciriola, small eel

ciuppin, thick fish (& vegetable) soup

civraxin, Sardinian large bread loaf

cocco/noce di cocco, coconut

cocktail di vongole, clam cocktail (clams, olive oil & lemon)

cocomero, watermelon

cocozelle, zucchini

coda, tail

coda alla vaccinara, oxtail stew in a tomato & garlic sauce

coda di bue, oxtail

coda di rospo, monkfish

coglioni di mulo, finely ground pork sausage threaded with a wide strip of lard. The name means "mule's balls"

cognac, cognac

colazione (prima), breakfast

collo, neck

colomba, dove-shaped cake. ***Colombo*** means pigeon

colombacchi, wild pigeon

coltello, knife

composta, stewed fruit (compote)

composta cotta, mixed cold, cooked vegetables

con, with

conchiglie, shell-shaped pasta. **Conchigliette** is a small version used in soup

condimento (i), condiment

confetti, sugared almonds (used in weddings & special occasions)

confettura, jam

con ghiaccio, on the rocks

coniglio, rabbit

coniglio all'agro, rabbit stewed in red wine

coniglio all'Anconetana, a stuffed-rabbit dish

cono, cone (as in ice cream cone)

Coniglio
Co-NEE-LEO

con seltz, w/soda

conserva, preserves/jam/jelly

conserva di frutta, preserves/jam/jelly

consommè, consomme (clear soup)

consommè madrilena, clear tomato soup

consommè reale, chicken consomme

contadina, alla, usually means served in a tomato & mushroom sauce (means "peasant woman")

conto, check/bill

contorno (i), side dish/garnish. This often refers to a vegetable side dish

contrafiletto/controfiletto, sirloin

copata, honey & nut wafer

coperto, cover charge

coppa, cup/goblet/small bowl. *Coppa* can also refer to smoked ham or smoked bacon

coppa di frutta, fruit cup/fruit cocktail

coppa di gamberetti, shrimp cocktail

coppa gelato, cup of ice cream/sundae

coratella di abbacchio, lamb heart, lung & liver dish

corda, lamb-tripe dish

cordulla, Sardinian dish made w/intestines

coregone, a type of salmon

coriandolo, coriander

cornetti, string beans

cornetto, croissant

corona, large white bean

Cornetto means trumpet

corposo, full-bodied wine

corretto, coffee or *espresso*
w/a shot of alcohol

Cortese, dry white wine

Corvo, dry, light white wine from Sicily

cosce di rana, frogs' legs

coscetta, leg/drumstick

coscia, leg

cosciette di rane, frogs' legs

casciotto, leg

casciotto di agnello, leg of lamb

casciotto di porcello, leg of young lamb

costa, rib/scallop

costa di manzo, rib roast/T-bone steak

costa di sedano, celery stalk

costarelle di abbacchio a scottadito, grilled lamb cutlet

costarelli, spareribs/pork chops

costata, chop/beef steak. *Costata di vitello* is a veal chop.
Costata di manzo is rib steak

costata alla fiorentina, grilled beef steak

costata alla pizzaiola, braised beef steak in a tomato sauce &
mozzarella cheese

costate, rib steaks

costate d'agnello, rack of lamb

costatella, rib steak

**costellata/costelleta/
costelletine,** rib steak

costicini, pork spareribs

costine, pork spareribs

costola arrostita, rib roast

costolatura, beef loin

costole di manzo, prime rib

costoletta (e), cutlet/chop (often coated in eggs & breadcrumbs
& fried in butter)

costoletta alla bolognese, breaded veal cutlet w/tomato sauce,
cheese & ham

costoletta alla milanese, breaded & fried veal cutlet

costoletta alla parmigiana, cutlet breaded & baked w/
parmesan cheese

costoletta alla siciliana, thin slices of veal or beef topped
w/chopped garlic & *parmesan* cheese, breaded & deep-fried

costoletta alla valdostana, cutlet w/ham & cheese stuffing

*We have found
that European
cuts of meat
often look
nothing like
cuts of the same
name in the States.*

costoletta alla viennese, wiener schnitzel
costoletta di vitello impanata, breaded veal cutlet
costolette di tonno, tuna steaks
costolette di vitello, veal chops
costolettine, lamb or pork chop
cotechino/coteghino, spicy pork sausage
cotognata, quince marmalade
cotogne, quince
cotoletta (e), cutlet, usually a veal cutlet
cotoletta alla bolognese, breaded veal cutlet topped w/ham,
 cheese & tomato sauce
cotto, cooked
cotto antico, bay leaf-flavored salami
cotto a puntino, medium done
courgette, zucchini
cozza (e), mussel
cozze alla marinara, mussels in white wine, garlic & parsley
cozze Posillipo, mussels in a spicy tomato sauce
crauti, sauerkraut
crema, cream/custard
crema caramella, custard w/caramelized-sugar topping
crema da montare, whipping cream
crema di, cream of
crema di funghi, cream of mushroom soup
crema di piselli, cream of pea soup
crema di pollo, cream of chicken soup
crema di verdura, puree of vegetables
crema fritta, fried-custard dessert
crema inglese, custard w/stewed fruit or cake
crème caramel, caramel custard
cremini, a type of mushroom
cremino, ice cream bar/a soft cheese
cren, horseradish
crescenza, a soft, buttery cheese (w/relatively low fat content)
crescionda, Umbrian dessert made from amaretto cookies,
 eggs, milk & unsweetened cocoa
crescione/crescione di fonte, watercress
crespelle, crêpes
crespelle alla fiorentina, spinach crêpes
crespolino, meat-filled pancake
croccheta (e), croquette
crocchette di patate, potato croquettes

Courgette is actually a french word found on menus near the french border.

51

crocchette di riso, deep-fried rice balls w/cheese in the center
crosta, crust (as in a pie crust)
crostaceo (i), shellfish
crostata, open-faced pie
crostata di frutta, fruit pie
crostini/crostoni, bread, fried or toasted in oil & topped
    w/many ingredients/croutons
crostini alla napoletana, toast w/cheese & anchovies
crostini alla provatura, toasted diced bread
    w/*provatura* cheese
crostini di mare, shellfish on fried bread
crostini di milza, toast w/veal paté
crostini Fiorentina, toast w/liver paté
crostini in brodo, croutons in broth
crostone di polenta, roasted meat (usually game) served on a
    round base of *polenta*
crudo, raw
crusca, bran. This also refers to a bread found in Ticino w/
    thick crust & dusted w/flour
cubbaita, nougat w/almonds, honey & sesame seeds
cucchiaio, spoon
cuccia, layered dish of slow-roasted meats, tomato sauce &
    grains. A specialty in Calabria
cucina, cuisine
culaccio, rump meat
culatello, ham cured in white wine
cumino, cumin
cunillu, Sardinian word for rabbit
cuoco, chef
cuore (i), heart
cuore di sedano, celery heart
cuori di carciofi, artichoke hearts
curry, curry
cuscusu di Trapani, couscous
Cynar, after-dinner drink made of artichokes
daino, deer
da portar via, to go
datteri di mare, mussels
dattero (i), date
decaffeinato, decaffeinated
del giorno, of the day
della casa, of the house

"cucina" means kitchen and cooking

"Decaffeinato" is becoming more common but be prepared for a condescending smile.

dente, al, pasta cooked until it's still slightly firm
   (means "to the tooth")
dentice, a Mediterranean fish (dentex) similar to sea bream
denti d'elefante, tubular pasta (like *macaroni*)
   (means"elephant's tooth")
di, of
diavola/diavolicchio, usually means served w/pepper or chili
   peppers. Can also mean a dish cooked over a flame since
   the terms mean "devil"
digestivo, after-dinner drink
disossata, boned rib steak
di stagione, in season
ditali, small tubular pasta for soup,
   often called thimbles. *Ditalini* is the
   smaller version of this pasta
diverso, varied
dolce (i), dessert/sweet/pastry. *Dolce* can also mean sweet wine
Dolcetto, fruity, dry red wine from Piedmont
dolci di Taglierini, sweetened noodle (taglierini) cake
dolcificante, artificial sweetener
dorato (a), browned/golden brown
Doria, alla, w/cucumbers
dragoncello, tarragon
e, and
eliche, spiral pasta.
   Often refered to as propellers
elicoidali, tubular pasta w/straight edges
emmenthal, Swiss cheese
empanata, breaded
entrecìte/entrecote di bue, boneless rib steak
erbazzone, vegetable pie
erbe, herbs
erbette, cooked greens
espresso, *espresso* (strong, small coffee)
espresso doppio, a double serving of *espresso*
espresso macchiato, *espresso* w/a small amount of foamy milk
on top. Compare this to *latte macchiato*
Est Est Est, a dry, semi-sweet white wine
Etna, red & white Sicilian wines
etto, fish dishes are frequently served by the *etto*
   (or 100 grams)
fagianella, bustard (bird)

diavolo-devil

*e means and.
é with an accent
means is.*

fagiano, pheasant

fagioli al fiasco, slow-cooked Tuscan bean dish served w/garlic, herbs & olive oil

fagioli alla maruzzara, beans in an oregano & tomato sauce

fagioli all'Uccelloto, white beans in a tomato sauce

fagioli bianchi, white beans

fagioli bianco di Spagna, lima beans

fagioli cannellini, small white beans

fagioli con le cotiche, beans in a tomato sauce w/slices of pork

fagioli cotti al forno, baked beans

fagioli freschi, fresh beans

fagioli lessati al forno, boiled baked beans

fagioli lessi, shelled, boiled beans

fagiolino (i) green bean/French bean

fagioli rampicanti, runner beans

fagioli rossi, red kidney beans

fagioli sgranati, fresh shelled beans

fagioli toscani, cooked white-bean dish

fagioli verdi, green beans

fagiolo (i), bean

fagottini, food wrapped around a filling

Falerno, dry white & red wines

fame, hungry

faraona, guinea fowl

farcito (a), stuffed

farfalle/farfallette, bow-tie or butterfly-shaped pasta

farfalline (i), bow-tie or butterfly-shaped pasta

farina, flour

farinata, baked pancake made from olive oil, chickpea flour, salt & pepper (eaten as a snack)

farricello, barley

farro, a type of wheat, similar to spelt

farsumagru, veal or beef roll stuffed w/ham, bacon, cheese, onions & parsley. A Sardinian specialty

fasolini, scallops

fatto in casa, homemade

fava (e), broad bean. Sometimes called *fave grande* or *fave España*

favarella, bean soup

favata, bean, sausage & bacon casserole

fave al Guanciale, broad beans cooked w/bacon & onions

fave e cicoria, pureéd fava beans, sauteéd chicory & olive oil. A specialty in Apulia

fegà, liver in Venice

fegatelli di maiale, pork liver

fegato (fegatini), liver.
Fegatini di maiale are pork livers; *fegatini di pollo* are chicken livers

fegato alla veneziana, liver & onions

fegato di vitello, calf's liver

Fernet, a bitter digestive liqueur

ferri, ai, sliced & grilled (means "on iron")

fesa, leg of veal

fesa in gelatina, roast veal w/aspic jelly

fetta di/fette di, slice of...

fettina, small slice

fettuccine (i), long, flat, thin ribbon noodle

fettuccine Alfredo, thin ribbon noodles w/cream, butter & nutmeg

fettuccine alla Panna, thin ribbon noodles w/cream, butter & nutmeg

fettuccine in brodo, noodle soup

fettuna, toasted or grilled over an open fire w/garlic & olive oil

fettura di melacotogne, quince jam

fiamma, alla, flamed

fiammifero (i), match

fianco, flank

fiasco, straw-covered bottle

fichi d'India/fichi indiani, prickly pears

fichi in sciroppo, figs in syrup

fichi mandorlati, figs stuffed w/almonds

fico (fichi), fig

fidelanza, spaghetti in tomato sauce in Liguria

filetti (di pomodoro), a sauce of sliced tomatoes

filetto (i), fillet or tenderloin

filu e ferru, Sardinian *grappa*

finferlo, an orange-colored mushroom

finocchiata, pork cured w/fennel & pepper

finocchio, fennel. *Finocchio selvatico* is wild fennel

finocchiona, fennel-flavored salami

fiocchetto, cold cut made from the leg of pork

fiocchi, flakes

[handwritten margin notes] liver in venice, liver in milwaukee... No grazie

[handwritten margin notes] fiasco. the old fashioned straw-covered bottle is really a novelty now.

fiocchi di granoturco, cornflakes
fiocco, ham shoulder
fior di latte, *mozzarella* made from cow's milk
fiore, flower
fiorentina, alla, w/oil, tomatoes & herbs
  (sometimes w/peas or spinach)
fiori con ripieno, stuffed zucchini flowers
fiori di zucca, zucchini flowers served either filled w/cheese,
  battered & fried or as a pizza topping
fiori di zucca fritti, fried zucchini flowers
flambé, flamed
focaccia, flat bread topped w/olive oil & sometimes cheese
  &/or onions. Can also mean cake
focaccia barese, stuffed pizza. A specialty of Apulia
focaccia di vitello, veal patty
foglia (e), leaf
foglia di alloro/foglia di lauro, bay leaf
foglia di vite, vine leaf
foiolo, tripe (stomach lining)
folpetto, the Venetian word for baby octopus
fondo di carciofo, artichoke heart
fonduta, melted cheese (fondue)
fontina, mild cheese (soft & creamy)
forchetta, fork
formaggini d'Alpe, cow's-milk cheese found in Ticino
formaggini di capra, fresh goat's-milk cheese found in Ticino
formaggio (formaggi), cheese
formaggio di fossa, aged sheep's-milk cheese
  from Le Marche
forno, al, baked
forte, strong
fracosta, rib steak
fragola (e), strawberry
fragole di bosco/fragoline di bosco, wild strawberries
fragolino, sea bream
fragolone, large strawberries
Frangelico, hazelnut-flavored cordial
frappé, milk shake
frascarelli, tiny *gnocchi*
Frascati, dry to slightly sweet white wine
frascota di bue, rib steak
frattaglie, giblets

foglia

fragolone

56

freddo (i)/fredda (e), cold/iced. *Tè freddo* is iced tea
fregolotta, flour, cornmeal & almond cake
fregula, dumpling soup
Freisa, dry to slightly sweet red wine
fresca (o), fresh/not cooked
freschi, wild mushrooms
fresco, al, outside (in the fresh air) *Freschi –*
FRESS - KEE
fricando, round of veal
fricassea, fricassee
fricò, cheese pancake
friggere, deep-fried (to deep fry)
frittata, omelette
frittata casalinga, plain omelette
frittata semplice, plain omelette
frittatina di patate, potato omelette
frittella (e), pancake/fritter
fritti ascolani, mixed fry of lamb chops, brains, olives
 & zucchini
fritto (a)/fritti (e), fried/deep-fried
fritto alla milanese, breaded & deep-fried
fritto alla napoletana, deep-fried fish, cheese & vegetables
fritto alla romana, deep-fried sweetbreads
fritto di verdura, fried vegetables
fritto misto, mixed deep-fried fish, meat or vegetables
fritto misto alla Fiorentina, meat & vegetable fritters
frittura, frying/fry
frittura del paese, mixed floured & fried seafood
frittura di pesce, mixed dish of fried small fish, squid &
 shrimp
frizzante, semi-sparkling wine
frolla, tender (meat)/flaky pastry *frizzante.*
frollini, biscuits
frullato, milk shake
frullato di frutta, fruit milk shake
frumento, wheat
frumentone, corn
frutta, fruit
frutta candita, candied fruit
frutta cotta, stewed fruit
frutta fresca, fresh fruit
frutta secca, dried fruit
frutti di bosco, berries

frutti di mare, seafood/seafood salad
fundador, w/brandy
funghetti, small mushroom-shaped pasta for soup
funghetto, al, sliced mushrooms cooked in garlic,
   onions & herbs
funghi trifolati, mushrooms sauteed in butter & garlic
fungo (funghi), mushroom
fuoco dell'Etna, strong, red Sicilian liquor
fusi, leg. *Fusi di pollo* is a chicken leg
fusilli, spiral-shaped pasta.
   Fusilli corti are short & *fusilli lunghi* are long
fusto, shank
galatina (in gelatina), pressed meat in aspic
galantina tartufata, truffles in aspic jelly
galletta, cracker/cookie. Can also refer to a mushroom or grape
galletto, chicken (cock)
Galliano, herb liqueur (yellow in color)
gallina, chicken (hen)
gallinaccio, woodcock/chanterelle mushroom
gallina faraona, guinea fowl
gallinella, waterfowl
gallinella faraona, guinea fowl
gallo, John Dory fish in Sicily
   (a firm-textured, white-fleshed
   fish w/a mild, sweet flavor
   & low fat content)
gallo cedrone, grouse (a game bird)
gamba, leg/drumstick/shank
gamba di vitello, veal shank
gamberelli, shrimp
gamberetta di rana, frogs' legs
gamberetto (i), shrimp
gambero (i), prawn/crayfish
gamberoni (gamberetti), large prawn
ganocchio, type of prawn
garetto, beef shank
garganelli, handmade pasta which is a square rolled into a tube
   (the dough is made from eggs, flour, grated *parmigiano*
   & nutmeg)
garofolato, beef stew
gaspaccio, gazpacho (the cold, tomato-based Spanish soup)
gasata/gassata, carbonated

galletto.

Gattinara, full-bodied red wine
gelatina, jelly/gelatine
gelato (i), ice cream/iced dessert
gelato al tartufo, ice cream w/chocolate sauce
gemelli, pasta made of two strands twisted
    around each other. The term means "twins"
genovese, alla, w/herbs
    (especially basil), olive oil
    & garlic/w/meat & onions
germe di grano, wheat germ
germinus, almond-meringue cookies
    from Sardinia
germogli, sprouts
gesuita, rib steak
ghiacciato, chilled/iced
ghiaccio, ice
ghianchetti, small anchovies
ghiotta, alla, grilled or roasted
ghiozzo, mackerel
giallo d'uova, egg yolk
gianchetti, small anchovies
gianduia, chocolate & hazelnut ice cream
gianduiotti, hazelnut-and-chocolate candies
giambonette(i)/giambonetto, boned chicken roll w/filling
giardiniera, small pieces of vegetables (a garnish)
gigantoni, large tubular pasta (means "giant")
gioddu, yogurt in Sardinia
giorno, del, of the day
gin, gin
ginepro, juniper berry
ginestrata, chicken & sweet wine soup (a sweet & sour soup).
    A Tuscan specialty
girarrosto, spit-roasted
girasole, sunflower
girello, rump
glassate, glazed
gnoccata al pomodoro, tomato pizza
gnocchetti, small *gnocchi*
gnocchetti alla Sarda/gnocchetti sarda, small pasta
    dumplings in various sauces. A specialty in Sardinia
gnocchi, flour or potato dumplings
gnocchi alla marchigiana, *gnocchi* w/chicken-giblet sauce

Handwritten margin notes: Genovese basil is considered the most fragrant. / gesuito means Jesuit... presumably because the priests got the best meat. / Good guess! / girasole means turns to the sun.

gnocchi alla piemontese, little balls of flour, egg & potato

gnocchi alla romana, semolina (flour) dumplings

gnocchi di patate, little balls of potato, flour & egg

gnocco fritto, deep-fried rolls of pasta

gnocco ingrassato, *focaccia* w/*prosciutto*

gnudi, means naked (w/out pasta). Stuffing
only, such as in ***ravioli gnudi***

gnudi... don't pronounce the G. NOO.DEE

gnumariddi, a sweetbread dish

gomiti, "c"-shaped tubular pasta

gomma da masticare, chewing gum

Kinda cute, hey?

gorgonzola, creamy, blue cheese (best-known Italian blue)

goulasch, goulash

graffo (i), doughnut

grana, mild, hard cheese (similar to *parmesan*)

granatina, steak tartare (raw ground beef). In most parts of
Italy this term means Italian ice or shaved ice

granceola, spider crab. A specialty of Venice

granchio (di mare), crab

granciporro (i), crab

grande, large

granello, seed

gran farro, wheat & bean soup. Also see *farro*

grani di, seeds of...

granita, coffee or fruit syrup served over crushed ice
(a "snow cone"). Originally made from snow from Mt. Etna

grano, wheat/corn

grano duro, duram wheat

grano padano, buttery, hard, seasoned cheese
w/a grainy texture

grano saraceno, buckwheat

granoturco/granturco, corn on the cob

granseola, a crab found in Venice

grappa, liquor made from grape pressings.
It's extremely strong

Grappa is a popular digestivo which can taste like heaven... or hell.

grappolo, a bunch
(as in a bunch of grapes)

grassi vegetali, vegetable oil

grasso (a), oily/fatty/fat/grease

graticola, grilled/broiled

gratin/gratinate, oven-browned w/cheese

gratinada, baked dish topped
w/grated cheese & breadcrumbs

gratis, free
grattugiato, grated
gratuito (a), free
gremolata, minced anchovies, parsely & lemon (used as a garnish)
grenadine, veal chunks (used in casserole dishes)
gricia, alla, w/bacon, onion, cheese & chili pepper
griglia, alla, grilled (usually charcoal grilled)
grigliata mista, mixed grill of meats or fish
Grignolino, high-quality red wine
grissino (i), long, thin bread stick
grongo/gruonco/grangu, conger eel
groppo, rump (meat)
groviera/groviera svizzera, sharp
    cheese w/holes (like Swiss cheese)

guancia.

guancia, pig's cheek. *Al guanciale* means cooked w/bacon &
    onions. Also refers to the delicacy of pig's cheek
guardaroba, coat room
guarnite, alla, served w/a garnish
guazzetto, usually refers to a stew (meat or fish). In Sardinia,
    this dish almost always contains capers
gubana, sweet bread roll (dried fruit & nut strudel found in
    Friuli-Venezia Giulia)
gulyas, beef stew found in Friuli-Venezia Giulia
gusti, flavors
hasce di manzo, hamburger patty
igname, yam
impanato (a), covered in breadcrumbs
impazzata di cozze/impepata di cozze, mussels cooked in
    their own juice w/black pepper, oil, parsley & garlic
incapriata, purée of fava beans & chicory
incasciata, layered dough, meat sauce, hard-boiled eggs, cheese
incluso (a), included
Indiana, all', w/curry (Indian style)
indivia, endive/chicory
indivia Belga, Belgian endive

insalata cotta...
Love it!

insaccati, salami
insalata, salad
insalata all'americana, shrimp & mayonnaise salad
insalata caprese, tomatoes, basil & *mozzarella* salad.
    Originally a specialty on the island of Capri, but now
    found everywhere in Italy
insalata cotta, cold, cooked vegetable salad

insalata di campo, field lettuce
insalata di cesare, Caesar salad
insalata di crudita, mixed raw vegetable salad
insalata di frutti di mare, seafood salad
insalata di funghi, raw mushroom salad
insalata di mare, seafood salad
insalata di patate, potato salad
insalata di petti di pollo, chicken salad w/walnuts
insalata di tonno, tuna salad
insalata di verdura cotta, boiled vegetable salad
insalata mista, mixed salad
insalata riccia, curly endive
insalata russa, diced potato & vegetable salad w/mayonnaise
insalata siciliana, salad featuring fennel & black olives
insalata verde, green salad
integrale, whole wheat
involtini al sugo, rolled veal cutlets w/ham & cheese & topped
   w/tomato sauce
involtini di cavolfiori, cabbage leaves stuffed w/meat
involtini di pesce, thin fish slices stuffed w/*prosciutto* & herbs
involtini di salvia, a deep-fried sage-leaf anchovy roll
involtini di vitello, veal roll usually stuffed w/salami & cheese
involtino (i), stuffed roll
iota, hearty vegetable soup (white beans, cabbage & bacon fat).
   A specialty of Trieste
Ischia, an island at the north end of the Gulf of Naples
I.V.A., abbreviation for Value Added Tax (V.A.T.)
jota, thick bean & sauerkraut soup (see Iota)
julienne, small strips of vegetables
kirsch, al, w/a clear cherry brandy
knoedel/knödeln, dumplings found in the
   Trentino-Alto Adige region
krapfen, doughnuts (Austrian name)
laccetto, mackerel
lacerto, mackerel
Lacrima Christi, popular red,
   white & rosé wines
Lago di Caldaro, light red wine
Lagrein Rosato, rosé wine
Lambrusco, well-known red wine (sweet)
lamelle di fegato, thin slices of liver sautéed in butter
lampasciuni, wild onions

Krapfen... sounds good!

Lacrima Christi - tears of Christ

lampone (i), raspberry

lampreda, lamprey (similar to an eel)

lanzado, mackerel

lardarellatta alla fiamma, larded & cooked on a grill

lardo, bacon/salt pork/lard

lardone, salt pork

lardoons, cured & fried pork

lardoso, meat fat

lasagne, thin layers of dough & meat, tomatoes, cheese & sauce (baked in the oven)

lasagne al forno, large strips of pasta cooked in sauce

lasagne alla portoghese, baked custard caramel

lasagne alla vincisgrassi, baked *lasagne* w/meatballs

lasagne verdi, spinach *lasagne*

latte, milk

latte al cacao, chocolate milk

latte di mandorla, almond milk

latte intero, whole milk

latte macchiato, steamed milk w/a small amount of *espresso*. Compare this to ***espresso macchiato***

latte magro, skim milk

latterini, poached fish dish

latte scremato, skim milk

latticini, small *mozzarella* balls

lattonzolo, suckling pig

lattuga (e), lettuce

lattuga romana, romaine lettuce

lauro, bay leaf

lavarello, a type of salmon

laziale, alla, w/onions

lecca-lecca, sucker/lollypop

leccia, pompano

leggero, light or weak/light wine

legume (i), vegetable

lenticchia (e), lentil

lepre, hare

lepre in salmì, marinated hare ("jugged hare")

leprotto, young hare

lessato (a), boiled

lesso, boiled. This can also refer to meat or fish stew

letterato, small tuna fish

lievito, yeast/baking powder

Lampreda.
Non grazie!

Latte.
generally not
drunk by
the glass.

lievito di birra, brewer's yeast

limonata

limonata, lemonade/lemon soda

limoncello, alcohol & lemon-zest drink. This is
  called *limoncino* in the Cinque Terre

limone (i), lemon. *Al limone* means w/lemon juice

lingua, tongue

linguine, flat noodles

liquore (i), liqueur. *Liquore Strega* is a sweet herb liqueur

liquoroso, fortified dessert wine

liscia/lisce, refers to smooth pasta (w/out ridges)

liscio, straight. *Brodo liscio* is plain broth

lissa, pompano in Venice

lista, menu. *Lista dei vini* is the wine list

livornese, alla, usually beans in tomato sauce w/celery
  & onions

locale, local

lodigiano, a type of *parmesan* cheese

Lombarda, alla, served fried in butter w/lemon juice & parsley

lombata, loin/leg. *Lombata di maiale* is a pork chop. *Lombata
  di vitello* is a grilled veal chop

lombata ai sassi, floured steak sautéed in butter w/sage & fried
  potatoes

lombatine, tenderloin or cut of meat for filet mignon

lombello, loin/leg

lombo di manzo, beef loin/sirloin

lombo di vitello, veal sirloin

lonza, loin

lucanica, spicy sausage

lucerna (e), grouper

luccio, pike

Lumaca

lucullo, alla, raw beef (steak tartare)

Lugana, dry white wine

luganega, pork sausage. This spicy sausage from Basilicata
  has many similar spellings such as *luganica* & *lucanica*

lumaca (lumache), snail. *Lumache* also refers to snail-shaped
  pasta. *Lumachine* is a small version of this pasta
  used in soup

lumache alla Bourguignonne, snails w/garlic butter
  ("Burgundy snails")

lunga, long (as in long pasta or *pasta lunga*)

lungo, lighter *espresso*

lupo di mare, sea perch

luvasu, sea bream
maccarello, mackerel
maccarones con bottarga, Sardinian pasta w/fish eggs
maccaruni di casa, Sicilian pasta dish served
  w/tomato & meat sauce
maccheroni, *macaroni*
maccheroni al pettine, pasta w/ridges usually served w/ragù
macchiato, *espresso* w/a small drop of milk
macco di fave, broad bean, onion & tomato soup
macedonia di frutta, fruit salad
macedonia di legumi, mixed cooked vegetables
macinata, ground. *La carne macinata* is ground beef
madera, al, cooked in Madeira wine
mafaldine, pasta ribbons
maggiorana, marjoram
magro, dish w/no meat/lean.
  Ravioli di magro is stuffed pasta
  w/herbs & *ricotta* cheese
maiale, pork
maionese, mayonnaise
mais, corn
malfatti di ricotta, *ricotta gnocchi. Malfatti* means badly
  made, a reference to the handmade dumplings in this dish
malloreddus, flavored dumplings found in Sardinia
malloreddus all'oristanese, saffron-flavored dumplings w/a
  sauce of Swiss chard, cream & eggs
maltagliata, *macaroni*
mammole, artichokes
mancia, tip
mandarino (i), tangerine/mandarin
mandorla (e)/mandorlata, almond
manicotti, stuffed (w/cheese & meats), baked pasta dish
mantecato, whipped ice cream. This also refers to a way to
  prepare cod
manzo (di bue), beef
manzo arrosto ripieno, stuffed roast
manzo lesso, boiled beef
manzo salato, corned beef
manzo stufato al vino rosso, beef stewed in red wine
maraschino/marasco, w/Maraschino (cherry-flavored liqueur)
marchigiana, alla, a dish in the style of Le Marche (one of the
  regions of Italy), usually cooked w/chicken giblet sauce

marjoram is a member of the oregano family.

mammole.

mare, di, of the sea

mare-monti, a dish served w/mushrooms & shrimp

margarina, margarine

margherita, this term is used to describe a pizza w/tomato, *mozzarella* & basil

marinara, alla, usually, but not always, means in tomato sauce (usually w/garlic & onions). The term means "of the sea" or "sailor's style," so can also refer to a dish w/seafood

marinata (o), marinated

maritozzo, soft bread roll

marmellata, marmalade/jam

marmellata d'arance, marmalade

marrone (i), chestnut. *Marrons glaces* are candied chestnuts

Marsala, fortified dessert wine from Sicily

marsala, al, in a Marsala (fortified dessert wine) sauce

Martini, vermouth

mascarpone, a soft, very creamy, fresh cheese (even for cheese, it's high fat)

masenette, tiny crabs eaten whole (w/the shell)/Venetian word for small soft-shelled crabs

matriciana, bacon, tomato & spices sauce

mattone, al, pounded flat (usually chicken) & roasted in a brick oven

mazza da tamburo, a parasol-shaped mushroom

mazzancelle/mazzancolle, very large prawns

mazzancougni, very large prawns

medaglione, medallions

medallione, a grilled ham & cheese sandwich

media, medium

mela (e), apple

melacotogna, quince

melagrana, pomegranate

melanzana (e), eggplant

melanzane al funghetto, sautéed eggplant

melanzane alla Napoletana, eggplant Neopolitan style (layered w/cheese & tomato puree & baked in an oven)

melanzane alla parmigiana, eggplant *parmesan* (w/tomatoes & *parmesan* cheese)

melanzane ripiene, stuffed eggplant

melassa, molasses

meliga, cornmeal

melone, melon/canteloupe

eggplant is a member of the same family as tomatoes, potatoes & peppers.

menta, mint
mentine, mints
menù, menu
menù a prezzo fisso, set menu
menù turistico, fixed-price menu
merca, roast fish dish from Sardinia
merenda, late morning/afternoon snack
meringa, meringue
meringa chantilly, meringue shells filled w/whipped cream
meringato/meringhe/meringua, meringue
merlango, hake/cod/whiting
merlano, whiting, cod or hake
merluzzo, cod
messicani, veal scallops dish/veal rolls
mesticanza, mixture of salad greens
metà, half
mezzo (a), half
mezzelune ai pinoli, pine-nut cookies from Umbria
mezze maniche, short tubular pasta
miascia, bread & fruit pudding
midollo, marrow
miele, honey
miglio, millet

millefoglie means a thousand leaves

milanese, alla, battered w/eggs & breadcrumbs & fried
Millefiori, herb-based liqueur
millefoglie, puff pastry/napoleon
millerighe, ridged tubular pasta (means "thousand lines"
   after the ridges in the pasta)
mimosa, spongecake & whipped-cream dessert
minerale, mineral (as in *acqua minerale* or mineral water)
minestra (minestre), soup (usually thick soup)
minestra al farro, soup made with *farro* (a wheat similar to
   spelt)
minestra di cipolle, onion soup
minestra di fagioli, bean soup
minestra di farina tostata, toasted-flour soup
minestra di farro, soup made with *farro* (a wheat)
minestra di funghi, cream of mushroom soup
minestra di lenticchie, lentil soup
minestra di pomodoro, tomato soup
minestra di riso, rice soup
minestra in brodo, broth w/noodles or rice & chicken livers

minestra maritata, meat broth & vegetable soup

minestre di piscialetto, dandelion-greens soup

minestrina, soup (usually clear)

minestrone, bean & vegetable soup w/noodles, vegetables, rice

minestrone alla genovese, vegetable soup
w/*macaroni* & spinach

minestrone verde, thick vegetable soup w/herbs & beans

mirabella (e), small plum

mirtillo (i), blueberry. The word *mirtilli* is also used for berries
in general & for cranberries

mischianza, salad of wild greens, herbs & edible flowers

misoltini, salted & dried shad (fish)

misticanza, salad of wild greens, herbs & edible flowers

misto/misti, mixed

misto del golfo/misto del paese, mixed floured & fried seafood

misto mare, mixed floured & fried seafood

mitilo, mussel

moka, mocha

molto, very

montanara, alla, has many meanings but generally means
w/red wine sauce or w/vegetables

montare, to whip (usually refers to cream)

montebianco/Mont Blanc, pyramid of sweetened chestnuts &
whipped cream (named after Mont Blanc)

Montepulciano, full-bodied, dry red wine

montone, mutton

monzittas, snails in Sardinia

mora (e), blackberry

Mont Blanc is the French side of Monte Bianco mountain.

mormora, small fish found in the Mediterranean

mortadella, luncheon meat w/pistachio nuts & peppercorns

morto, pot roast

mosca, con la, a drink (usually *Sambuca*) served "w/the
fly"(*con la mosca*). The "fly" is a coffee bean in the glass

moscardino (i), small squid

Moscatello/Moscato, muscatel (table & dessert white & red
wines from the muscat grape)

mostarda, mustard. This word is rarely used. Most use *senape*

mostarda di frutta, candied fruits in syrup/preserved fruits in
a mustard sauce/fruit chutney

mousse al cioccolato, chocolate mousse

mozzarella, a soft, fresh (unripened), slightly sweet cheese

mozzarella di bufala, *mozzarella* made from buffalo milk

mozzarella in carrozza, fried *mozzarella* sandwich
  (means "in a carriage")
muddica, breadcrumbs in Sicily
muggine, grey mullet
muscoletti, shank
muscoli, mussels. This word is rarely used. Most use *cozze*
muscoli alla marinara, steamed mussels dish
musetto, salami
napoletana, ("Naples-style") w/tomato sauce (w/out meat)
nasello, whiting/hake/cod
naturale, plain/natural
nave, di, w/seafood
navone (i), turnip
`nduja, Calabrian pork sausage
Nebbiolo, full-bodied dry red wine
nepitella, an herb similar to mint
nero (a), black
nervetti, calf's foot dish (tendons of calves' feet).
  A Venetian specialty
nespola, medlar (a tart fruit)
nidi di rondine, pasta rolls
nocciola (e), hazelnut
noccioline americane, peanuts
nocciole, nuts
noce (i), nut/walnut. Can also refer to the top round of veal
noce di cocco, coconut
nocelli, walnut-raisin cookies
noce moscata, nutmeg
nocepesca, nectarine
noci d'anacardo, cashews
Nocillo/Nocino, liquor made from walnuts
nodino (i), chop/small grilled pork chop
non, not
non fumatori, no smoking
non gassata, still or not carbonated
nonna, alla, this can be any sauce served w/pasta. The term
  means "grandmother" & there are as many variations of
  "alla nonna" as there are grandmothers
norcina, sausage & cheese sauce. After the town of Norcia
Norma, alla, this usually refers to a dish served w/eggplants,
  tomatoes, basil & sometimes *ricotta* cheese
nostrale/nostrano, home-grown/local

[handwritten margin note: Navone.]

[handwritten margin note: nervetti... I don't think so.]

novellame, a spread of salted anchovies & *peperoncino* sauce
novello/novelli, fresh/tender
o, or
oca, goose
occhiate, orata (a fish)
occhi di lupo, small tubular pasta
   "wolves' eyes")
olio, oil/olive oil
olio d'arachide, peanut oil
olio da tavola, salad oil
olio di cartamo, safflower oil
olio di girasole, sunflower oil
olio di grano/olio di granturco, corn oil
olio di palma, palm oil
olio di semi, seed oil/corn oil
olio d'oliva, olive oil
olio santo, chili-infused oil
oliva (e), olive (*nere*, black, *verdi,* green)
olive agrodolci, olives in sugar & vinegar
olive ascolane, large green olives. *Olive all'ascolana,*
   in Le Marche, olives stuffed w/meat & fried in olive oil
ombra, glass of wine in Venice. This word is usually used at a
   bar & not at a restaurant
ombrina, umbrine (seafood/bass)
omelette, omelette
omelette casalinga, plain omelette
omelette semplice, plain omelette
oranciata, orangeade
orata, a fish found in the Mediterranean (bream/gilthead)
oratino, a small *orata* fish
orecchiette, small ear-shaped pasta
orecchiette con le cime di rapa, small ear-shaped pasta
   w/turnips. A specialty in Apulia
origano, oregano
ortaggi, vegetables/greens/herbs
Orvieto, light, dry, white wine from Orvieto in Umbria
orzata, almond or barley-flavored water
orzetto, barley & potato soup
orzo (i), rice-shaped pasta. Can also refer to barley
osso, bone
ossobuco (ossibuchi), braised veal-shank dish. You may be
   given a marrow spoon to eat the marrow in the bone

Olio d'oliva
we never leave
Italy without
a bottle

ossobuco alla milanese, veal shank, tomatoes, garlic & wine

ostrica (ostriche), oyster

ovalina, a type of *mozzarella* cheese

ovolo (i), a rare (& delicious) mushroom w/an orange & scarlet color. Sometimes called Caesar's mushroom

pacchetto, package

paciugo, parfait

padella, in, fried

paesana, alla, usually means served w/bacon (or sausage), potatoes, carrots & other vegetables

paeta, spit-roasted turkey

pagaro/pagello, sea bream/porgy

paglia e fieno, pasta dish w/yellow (egg) & green (spinach) pasta (means "straw & hay")

pagliarino, soft, mild cheese

pagliata, a dish containing organ meat

pagnotta, loaf

pagnotta del cacciatore, game birds roasted in dough

pagro, sea bream/porgy

paiata, spit-roasted turkey

paillard, beef rib steak or veal cutlet pounded thin & grilled

pajata, a dish containing organ meat

palamito, bonito fish

palemone, prawns

pallina, scoop (as in scoop of ice cream). The word really means "marble"

palomba/palombaccia, pigeon

palombacci, an Umbrian dish of small birds cooked whole on a spit

palombo, dogfish/shark found in Sicily

panafittas, dried bread broken into pieces & boiled (like pasta), then served in a tomato sauce in Sardinia

panardo, a thirty-course feast served in Abruzzo

panata, bread soup

pancetta, bacon (cured pork belly)

pancetta arrotolata, rolled bacon flavored w/cloves

pan có Santi, sweet bread w/raisins, dates, honey & walnuts. "Saints' bread" is eaten around All Saints Day (November 1)

pan di Genova, almond cake

[handwritten annotation: palomba. They're all over the down place.]

pan di Spagna, spongecake

pandolce, cake w/dried fruit

pandoro (di Verona), star-shaped light cake w/sugar topping

pane, bread/loaf

pane bianco, white bread

pane bigio, whole-wheat bread

pane carasau, flat crispy bread found in Sardinia. Also known
as *carta da musica* (music paper)

pane di segale, rye bread

pane e coperto, the charge for bread & for sitting at the table

pane frattau, *pane carasau* topped w/tomato sauce, grated
cheese & a fried egg. A specialty in Sardinia

pane grattugiato, breadcrumbs

pane integrale, whole-wheat bread

panelle, chickpea fritters

pane nero, dark bread

pane pepato, gingerbread

pane piccante, gingerbread

pane scuro, pumpernickel bread

pane toscano, sourdough bread

pane tostato, toast

panettone, spiced cakes or
coffeecakes w/candied fruits

panforte, flat, hard fruitcake

pan grattato, breadcrumbs

panicielli d'uva passula, grapes wrapped in leaves & baked

panino (i), roll/sandwich

panino imbottito, sandwich

paniscia, rice, sausage & bean soup

pan matteloch, honey bread found in the lake country

pan meino, cornmeal bread/cake (millet bread) w/elderflowers

panna, cream

panna, alla, served in a cream sauce or w/creamy gravy

panna, con, in a cream sauce/w/cream

panna cotta, rich cream custard

panna da montare/panna montata, whipped cream

pannocchia, corn on the cob

panpepato, gingerbread or hazelnut cake

pansoti/pansotti, triangular-shaped filled pasta

pan tostato, toast

panzanella, bread & vegetable salad

panzerotti, baked (or deep-fried) dough filled w/pork, cheese,
tomatoes or other ingredients

*Pane.
the Italians,
like the French,
are fiercely
proud of their
bread.*

panzoni, stuffed ravioli dish

paparot, cornmeal & spinach dish from Friuli-Venezia Giulia

pappa al pomodoro, tomato & bread soup

pappardelle, long, flat, wide pasta

pappardelle al sugo di lepre/pappardelle alla lepre, strips of pasta w/rabbit sauce

paprica, paprika

pardulas, Sardinian pastries filled w/cream cheese

parigina, hamburger buns. In Sicily, this refers to bread

parmigiana, alla, w/*parmesan* cheese & tomatoes

parmigiana di melanzane, baked slices of eggplant layered w/*parmesan* cheese, tomatoes & *mozzarella*

parmigiano, *parmesan* cheese usually served grated

parmigiano-reggiano, the "real" name for *parmesan* cheese

partenopea, means "Naples' style," the same as *Napolitana*

Pasqualina, "Easter style" which can mean roasted in an oven w/olive oil, onion, garlic, black olives & celery. *Torta Pasqualina* is a pie featuring artichokes

passate di legumi, puree of vegetables

passatelli, pasta of *parmesan* cheese, eggs & breadcrumbs

passato, puree

passato di verdura, cream of vegetable soup

passera di mare, flounder

passera pianuzza, flounder

passerino, flounder

pasta, pasta (dough made of flour, oil, butter, eggs & water). The first course in Italy. If you find -*ette* or -*ini* after pasta, this means a smaller version of pasta. For example, *pennette* & *pennini* are smaller versions of *penne.* If you find -*oni* after pasta, this means a large pasta like *rigatoni. Pasta* that starts w/*taglia* is made of long, thin strips. *Pasta* can also mean pastry

pasta al forno, any pasta mixed w/a sauce & baked

pasta alla Norma, pasta w/tomatoes, basil & eggplant topped w/*ricotta* cheese

pasta asciutta, any pasta not eaten in soup

pasta con le sarde, pasta w/fresh sardines

pasta d'arachide, peanut butter

pasta di olive, olive paste

pasta e ceci, pasta & chickpea soup

pasta e fagioli, pasta & bean soup

pasta frolla, puff pastry
pasta in brodo, pasta in broth
pasta 'ncasciata, pasta baked w/eggplant, salami, tomato/basil
pasta reale (paste reali), marzipan cake
 (means "royal pastry")
pasta sfoglia, puff-pastry dough
paste, pastries
pastella, batter for frying
pasticceria (e), pastry
pasticcetti, small tarts
pasticciata, baked pasta (in a casserole)
pasticcini da te, teacakes/small pastries
pasticcino (i), cake/small pastry/tart
pasticcio, pastry/pie. Also the Venetian word for baked lasagne
pasticcio di maccheroni, sweet pie containing meat sauce
pastiera napoletana, *ricotta* cheese-filled pastry
pastina, small pasta usually used in soup
pastina in brodo, pasta served in soup
pastissa, pot pie
pasto, meal
patata (e), potato
patate al lesso, boiled potatoes
patate al ghiotto/patate alla ghiottona, stuffed baked potatoes
patate americane, sweet potato
patate arroste, roasted potatoes
patate bollite, boiled potatoes
patate dolci, sweet potato
patate fritte, fried potatoes/french fries
patate in padella, potatoes fried in a pan
patate lesse, boiled potatoes
patate novelle, new potatoes
patate rosolate, roasted potatoes
patate saltate, potatoes sliced & sautéed
patate tenere, new potatoes
patatine fritte, french fries/chips
patatine novelle, small roasted potatoes
pate/paterini, pâté
pecora, sheep/ewe
pecorino, hard, sharp cheese usually served grated.
 Pecorino alla griglia is a Sardinian specialty of grilled
 pecorino cheese
pellegrine, scallops

[handwritten marginal note: Anti - before / Pasto - meal / antipasto.]

penne, tube-shaped pasta (cut at an angle)

pennette, smaller version of *penne*

penneziti, larger version of *penne*

pennoni, the largest version of *penne*

peoci, mussels. Also the Venetian word for "head lice"

pepata di cozze, mussels in a black pepper, oil & garlic sauce

pepato, peppered

pepe, black pepper

pepe di Giamaica, allspice

peperonata, tomatoes, peppers & onion stewed together

peperoncino (i), small, spicy pickled pepper

peperone (i), pepper

peperoni alla brace, roasted marinated peppers

peperoni imbottiti, stuffed peppers

peperoni ripieni, stuffed peppers

peperoni rossi, red peppers

peperoni sott'aceto, pickled chilis

peperoni verdi, green peppers

pera (e), pear

perciatelli, hollow spaghetti noodles

per contorno, meal includes salad or side dish

pere helene/pere elena, poached pear served in vanilla ice cream & topped w/chocolate sauce

pernice, partridge

persico, perch

pesca (pesche), peach

pesca melba, peaches in syrup w/ice cream & whipped cream

pescatora/pescatore, seafood sauce for pasta & rice dishes

pescatrice, angler fish

pesce, fish

pesce carpionata, marinated fish in herbs

pesce in saor, fish in a sauce of onion, raisin, pine nut & vinegar. A specialty in Veneto

pesce persico, perch

pesce San Pietro, John Dory fish (a firm-textured, white-fleshed fish w/a mild, sweet flavor and low fat content)

pesce sciabola, an eel-like fish

pesce serra, bluefish

pesce spada, swordfish

pesce stocco, cod

pesce turchino, mackerel

pesche, peaches

pesche aurora, spongecake soaked in peach liqueur

pesto, basil, oil, garlic & pine-nut sauce

petonchio, scallops

petroniana, alla, can mean many things, most frequently
breaded & fried & topped w/melted cheese

pettine (i), small scallop

petto, breast (of poultry)

petto alla principessa, chicken floured & fried in butter &
served w/an egg on top

petto all'arancio, chicken in an orange sauce

petto di pollo, chicken breast

peverada, chicken liver & anchovy sauce *only for the brave.*

pezzenta, pork salami

pezzo, piece

piacere, of your own choice (your pleasure)

piadina, soft, flat bread

pianuzza, flounder/halibut

piastra, grilled on a flat steel plate

piattino, saucer

piatto (i), dish/plate. *Piatti freddi* means cold dishes

piatto del giorno, dish of the day

piccante, highly seasoned (hot)

piccata (e), veal scallop

piccata all'allegro, veal scallop fried in butter w/lemon juice

piccata alla Lombarda, veal scallop fried in butter w/lemon
juice & parsley

piccata di vitello, veal cooked in lemon & parsley

piccatina, veal scallop dish

piccioncino, young pigeon

piccione, pigeon

piccione selvatico, wild pigeon

piccolo (i)/piccola (e), small

pici, eggless pasta

piede (i), foot

piemontese, sauce w/truffles ("Piedmont style")

pietanza, dish/main course

pignata, lamb or goat w/herbs. A specialty from Basilicata
named after the terra-cotta pot it's cooked in

pimento, pimento/allspice

pimiento, sweet red peppers

pinoccate/pinocchiata, almond & pine-nut cake

pinolata, pine-nut dessert cake found in Tuscany

pinolo (i), pine nut
Pinot Grigio, light, fruity white wine
pinsimonio/pinzimonio, oil, pepper & salt dressing/oil &
    mustard dressing for dipping
pinza, yellow flour, pine nut & raisin cake from Veneto
pipe, pasta similar to *lumache* (a snail-shaped pasta)
pisello (i), pea
pistacchi, pistachio nuts
pitta, pizza either stuffed or
    topped with many ingredients.
    Popular in Calabria
piviere, plover (bird)
pizza, pizza
pizza alla marinara, the "true"
    pizza: tomato, olive oil & oregano
pizza alla napoletana, pizza w/cheese, capers, tomatoes,
    anchovies, olives & *mozzarella*
pizza alla siciliana, pizza w/salami or ham, anchovies, olives,
    tomatoes & *mozzarella*
pizza bianca, pizza bread topped w/sea salt & olive oil
pizza capricciosa, same as *pizza quattro stagioni*
pizza di Pasqua, cheese bread
pizzaiola, w/tomato & garlic sauce
pizzaiolo, pizza man (the maker of pizzas)
pizza margherita, pizza w/tomato, basil & *mozzarella*
pizza marinara, pizza w/garlic, oil & oregano. Can also refer
    to a pizza w/black olives, anchovies, tomatoes & capers
pizza quattro stagioni, w/seafood, cheese,
    artichokes & ham in four sections.
    Means "four seasons" & is a pizza which has a
    different topping for each quarter
pizza rustica, common in central Italy; serves large rectangular
    pizzas with thicker crusts and more toppings than usually
    found in a *pizzeria.* You can order as much as you want, and
    pay by weight
pizzelle, small (fried) pizzas
pizzetta, small pizza
pizzoccheri, pasta made w/buckwheat flour
polenta, cornmeal mush
polenta concia, *polenta* w/cheese
polenta di grano saraceno, buckwheat *polenta*
polenta dolce, sweet *polenta* dessert

Pizza... Man's highest culinary achievement.

polenta e osei, *polenta* w/roast fowl

polenta grassa, butter, fontina cheese & *polenta*

polenta pasticciata, *polenta* served w/meat sauce, cheese, mushrooms & sauce (*polenta* pie)

polipetto (i), small squid/baby octopus

polipo (i)/polpo (i), octopus

pollame, poultry

pollastra/pollastrello, young chicken

pollo al mattone is a favorite!

pollo al mattone/pollastrino al mattone, chicken pounded flat & roasted in a brick oven

polletto, spring chicken

pollo, chicken

pollo alla diavola, highly spiced, grilled chicken

pollo alla Marengo, sautéed chicken dish with many ingredients (usually tomatoes, mushrooms & onions). The dish takes its name from the town of Marengo, where Napoleon defeated the Austrians

pollo alla romana, fried chicken pieces, bacon & garlic

pollo all'arrabbiata, "Enraged chicken" (a spicy chicken dish)

pollo arrosto, roasted chicken

pollo fritto Fiorentina, chicken marinated in oil, lemon juice & herbs

pollo in bellavista, roasted chicken dish w/vegetables

pollo novello, spring chicken

pollo piccata al Marsala, chicken pounded thin & fried in butter & Marsala wine

pollo scarpariello, boneless chicken w/lemon, garlic & parsley

polpa, lean meat/flesh

polpetielle, baby octopus

polpetta (e) di carne, meatball

polpetti affogati, small octopuses cooked w/tomatoes (means "drowned octopuses")

polpettine (i), meatball. *Polpettine di pesce* is a seafood ball

polpettone, meat loaf

polpi arricciati, "curled octopus." An octopus dish in which the octopus is curled by beating & twirling it in a basket

polpo, octopus

polpo in purgatorio, octopus sautéed in oil w/tomatoes & peppers

pomi d'oro, the original name for tomato (means "golden apple"). It's believed that the tomato arrived in Europe w/a golden color that turned red under the hot Mediterranean sun

pommarola (salsa di), tomato sauce

pomo (i), apple

pomodoro (i), tomato

pomodoro, al, w/tomato sauce

pomodoro doppio (concentrato), thick tomato paste

pomodoro pelati, peeled tomatoes in their own juice

pomodoro pumate, sun-dried tomato

pomodoro super cirio, thick tomato pureé

pomodori con tonno, tomatoes stuffed w/tuna

pomodori secchi, sun-dried tomatoes

pompelmo, grapefruit

popone, melon

porcecellino, suckling pig

porceddu/porcheddu, Sardinian word for roast suckling pig

porcello, young pig

porchetta, roast suckling pig stuffed w/herbs

porcini, mushrooms (the wild mushroom boletus)

porco, pork

porri dorati, battered & deep-fried leeks

porro (i), leek

portacenere, ashtray

portafoglio, veal cutlet stuffed w/herbs, cheese & other ingredients. This is also the word for wallet

porta cenere Can't get away from it in Italy.

portata (e), course

porto, port

portoghese, usually means w/tomato sauce

porzione, portion

posillipo, seafood sauce

praio, dorade (fish)/gilt-head bream

pranzo, lunch/dinner

presnitz, dessert made w/dried fruit from Fruili-Venezia Giulia

prezzemolo (i), parsley

prezzo, price

prezzo fisso, fixed price

prima colazione, breakfast

primavera, spring vegetables & cream sauce

primizie, spring vegetables or fruit

primo, first (as in *primo piatto*, first course)

principale, main (as in *piatto principale*, main course)

profiterole, filled ice-cream puff topped w/chocolate sauce &
   whipped cream
prosciutto, aged & cured ham
prosciutto affumicato, cured, smoked ham
prosciutto cotto, cooked or boiled ham
prosciutto crudo, salted, cured ham/Parma ham
prosciutto di cinghiale, smoked wild boar
prosciutto di San Daniele, a cured ham
   named after a town in the Friuli-Venezia Giulia region
prosciutto e melone, ham & melon
prosciutto di Parma, Parma ham
   (famous cured ham of Parma)
prosecco, sparkling white wine from Veneto
provatura, soft, mild & sweet cheese
provenzale, onions, black olives, tomato & mushroom sauce
provolone, mild buffalo cheese
provolone dolce, mild, white, medium-hard cheese
provolone piccante, sharp cheese
prugna (e), plum
prugna secca (prugne secche), prune
pumaruolo/pumaruoro, tomato in Sicily & Campania
pumate, sun-dried tomatoes
punta di vitello, veal brisket
puntarelle, a salad green
punte di asparagi, asparagus tips
Punt e Mes, orange-flavored vermouth
   (drunk before meals)
puntino, a, medium done
punto, breast. *Punto* also means medium rare
purea, pureed/mashed
purea di fave, a puree of broad beans
   often spread on bread
purè di patate, mashed potatoes
puttanaio, a stew-like ratatouille
   (means "prostitute stew")

Absolut favorite

puttanesca, tomato, black olives, anchovies, capers & garlic
   sauce (the term means "prostitute"). Allegedly named
   because prostitutes could prepare this quick meal between
   "customers"
quadrello, pork loin
quadrello d'agnello, rack of lamb
quadretti, refers to small squares of pasta

quadrucci, square-shaped pasta for soup
quaglia (e), quail
quattro formaggi, four cheeses
quattro spezie, four spices combined
  (pepper, cloves, juniper & nutmeg)
quattro stagioni, pizza
  w/seafood, cheese,
  artichokes & ham
  in four sections

Quattro Stagione
means
Four Seasons

rabarbaro, rhubarb. This can also refer to an
  after-dinner liqueur
radiatori, pasta shaped like a radiator
radicchio, red endive/red chicory (bitter red lettuce)
rafano, horseradish
ragnetto, rolls
ragno, sea bass
ragno di mare, spider crab
ragù, tomato-based meat sauce
ragusano, hard, slightly sweet cheese
ramolaccio, horseradish
ranapescatrice, angler fish
rane, frogs or frogs' legs
rannocchi, frog or frogs' legs
rapa (e), turnip
rape rosse, beet root
raspante, farm-raised (usually chicken). Means "scratching"
Ratafia, black-cherry liqueur
rattatuia, ratatouille
ravanada, horseradish sauce
ravanello (i), radish
raviggiolo, goat's-milk cheese
ravioli, squares of pasta w/stuffing. *Raviolini* are half-circle
  stuffed pasta
ravioli gnudi, ravioli stuffing (without the pasta)
ravioli verdi, spinach ravioli
razza, ray
recchie/recchietelle, the word in Apulia for *orecchiette* (ear-
  shaped pasta)
remolazzitt, radish
rene (i), kidney
ribes, currants
ribes neri, black currants

Rana.

ribes rossi, red currants

ribollita, vegetable soup (which means "reboiled") thickened
w/bread. There are many versions of this Tuscan soup

ricciarelli, marzipan &/or almond biscuits

riccio (di mare)/ricci (di mare), sea urchin

ricciola, amberjack (fish)

riccioli, small, curly pasta

riccolo, curly endive

ricotta, similar to cottage cheese, sweetened when
used in desserts

ricotta al maraschino, *ricotta* cheese w/maraschino

rigaglia (e), giblets

rigata (e), refers to ridges in pasta

rigatoni, large tube-shaped pasta (always has ridges)

rigatoni alla Norma, a Sicilian dish of pasta w/eggplant &
tomato sauce

righini, bluegill

ripieno/ripiene, stuffed

riserva, mature wine

risi e bisi, creamy rice w/green peas.
Bisi is the Venetian word for peas

riso (i), rice

riso ai gamberi, rice w/shrimp

riso alla genovese, rice w/sauce of minced beef (or veal)
w/vegetables

riso alla Greca, rice, vegetables & sausage dish (Greek style)

riso alla milanese, golden rice dish from Milan
featuring saffron

riso alla pilota, rice w/a sausage meat sauce

riso e ceci, broth of rice & chickpeas w/tomatoes & spices

riso in bianco, white rice w/butter

riso in cagnone, boiled rice topped w/*parmesan* cheese

riso mantecado, rice cooked in butter & milk

riso nero, black rice. The rice is made black from squid ink

risoni, rice-shaped pasta for soup

risotto, creamy rice dish w/various ingredients. Served as a
first course, *i primi,* after the *antipasto*

risotto ai fiori di zucca, rice dish made w/a heavy cream base
& zucchini flowers stirred in w/*parmesan.* A Ticino specialty

risotto alla certosina, creamy rice dish w/shrimp, mushrooms,
peas & sometimes frogs' legs

risotto alla mantovana, rice dish w/salami & *parmesan* cheese

Ribollita means Reboiled.

Risi e Bisi... another favorite.

risotto alla milanese, rice w/butter, saffron, beef,
   zucchini & *parmesan*

risotto alla pescatora, spicy rice w/seafood

risotto alla romana, rice usually w/lamb & potatoes

risotto alla valdostana, rice w/cheese & wine

risotto alla Valenciana, the same dish as Spanish *paella*

risotto alla Veneta, rice w/mussels

risotto alla veronese, rice & ham w/mushrooms

risotto al salto, crisp rice cake

risotto di frutti di mare, rice w/shellfish

risotto di peoci, rice w/mussels

risotto nero, black *risotto.*
   Squid or cuttlefish ink makes the rice black

ristretto, reduced broth

robiola, soft, mild & slightly sweet cheese

robiolina, sheep's-milk cheese

rocciate, pastry w/fruit & nuts

rognoncini, kidneys

rognoncini al vino bianco, kidneys in white-wine sauce

rognone (i), kidney

rolatine di vitello, veal cutlets stuffed w/ham &/or cheese

rollè, roll

romagnola, typically, a sauce of tomato, garlic & parsley

romana, alla, a catch-all term that literally means
   "Roman style"

rombo, turbot

rosato, rosé

rosbif, roast beef

roscioli, red mullet in Abruzzo

rosé, rosé (blush) wine

rosmarino, rosemary

Rosolio, sweet liqueur

rospo, monkfish/angler fish. *Rospo* also means toad,
   so this fish is often referred to as *pesce rospo*

rosso, red

Rosso Antico, cherry-flavored vermouth

rotella, round

rotelle/rotelline, wheel-shaped pasta

rotini, spiral-shaped pasta

rotolo, rolled meat w/stuffing.
   Rotolo di spinaci is a spinach roll (pasta w/spinach)

rovi, blackberries

rucola, arugula, also called rocket salad

rughetta, salad green

rujolos, Sardinian sweet-cheese fritters

rum, rum

ruote di carro, pasta in the shape of a wheel (same as *rotelle*)

rustica, alla, usually means a pepper & olive sauce, but can mean many things

sagro, sea bream

salame (i), smoked sausage. *Salamino* is a small salami

salame di cioccolato/ salame al cioccolato, chocolate cake in the shape of (& looks like) a salami

salamino piccante, pepperoni

salatina, greens for salad

salatini, crackers/snacks

salato, salted/salami

salciccia, sausage

sale, salt

salmi, in, marinated in wine, garlic & herbs (usually w/game)

salmone, salmon. *Salmoncino* is young salmon

salsa, sauce. *Salsa balsamella* is béchamel (white) sauce

salsa bianca, white sauce

salsa di pommarola, tomato sauce

salsa di salsiccie, sausage sauce

salsa per la cacciagione, "hunters' sauce" for cooking game

salsa tartara, tartar sauce

salsa verde, parsley-based green sauce (w/oil, lemon juice, capers & garlic)

salsicce di maiale, pork sausages

salsiccia (e), fresh sausage

saltato (i)/saltata (e), sautéed

saltimbocca, veal cutlet wrapped around ham & sage

salumi, sausages

salumi cotti, cooked sausages & cured meats

salvia, sage

salvietta, napkin (paper)

Sambuca, anise-flavored liqueur. When served *con la mosca* ("w/the fly"), the "fly" is a coffee bean in the glass

sanato, young calf

sandwich, sandwich

sangiovese, primary grape of Chianti wine

sangue, al, rare

Sanguinaccio, blood sausage (black pudding).
Also a chocolate spread made from chocolate & pigs' blood
San Pietro, John Dory fish (a firm-textured, white-fleshed fish
w/a mild, sweet flavor and low fat content)
San Severo, dry red wine from southern Italy
saor, sweet & sour sauce
sapa, thick sauce made from the juice of freshly pressed grapes
saporito (a), mild/tasty
sarago (saraghi), bluegill
sarda (e)/sardine, sardine
sarda, alla, tomato & meat sauce w/herbs & red wine
("Sardinian style")
sarde a beccaficu, sardines usually stuffed w/pine nuts &
raisins. A Sicilian specialty
sardella, fried baby fish minced w/olive oil & powdered
peppers from Calabria
sardina, small sardine
sardo, hard, aromatic cheese
sardoncini, little sardines
sartù, baked rice dish w/tomatoes, meatballs & mushrooms
savarin, cake baked in a ring mold & soaked in liquor. The
center is filled w/fruit & whipped cream
sbrisolona, flour, cornmeal & almond cake (crumble cake)
scalogno (i), shallot
scaloppa, veal scallop (thin slices of veal)
scaloppa alla fiorentina, veal scallop w/spinach & white sauce
scaloppa milanese, breaded, fried veal scallop
scaloppa napoletana, veal scallop coated in breadcrumbs
scaloppina (e), veal scallop
scaloppine alla boscaiola, veal scallops sautéed in oil & butter
& served w/an herb, black olive & onion sauce
scaloppine alla campagnola, veal scallops served in a sauce.
The term means "rustic"
scaloppine al marsala, small veal scallops in marsala wine
scaloppine al vino bianco, small veal scallops in
white-wine sauce
scamorza, mild cheese (aged *mozzarella*)
scampi, shrimp/prawns
scampi all'Americana, shrimp in a tomato sauce
scanello, sirloin
scapece, fried fish in vinegar & saffron/fried vegetables which
are then marinated

scarda, bream (fish)

scarola, escarole (a crispy leaf lettuce)

scarpaccia, zucchini pie (means "old shoe")

scarpena, scorpion fish

scelta, of your choice

schiacciata, flat bread (means "squashed flat")

schila, shrimp in Venice

schmarren, crêpes w/fruit & cream from Trentino-Alto Adige

scialatielli, wide noodles

scialcione, bread loaf

sciroppato (a), cooked in syrup

sciroppo, syrup

sciroppo d'acero, maple syrup

scodella, bowl

scorfano, scorpion fish

scorfano rosso, scorpion fish

scodella

scorze d'amelle, pasta shaped like slivered almonds found in Basilicata

scorzonera, salsify

scotch, scotch

scottadito, grilled lamb chops

scottiglia di cinghiale, wild-boar chops

scrippelle, omelettes cut into thin strips & served in a meat broth. A specialty in Abruzzo & Molise

sebadas, bread filled w/cheese & honey, then fried. A Sardinian specialty

secco (a), dry. ***Funghi secchi*** are dried mushrooms

secondo piatto, second course

sedani, the name for a small pasta similar to *rigatoni*

sedano, celery

sedano rapa, celery root

segale, rye

sella, saddle

selvaggina, game/venison

semente/semenza/senze, seeds

semi di, seeds of...

semi di melone, pasta noodle for soup in the shape of melon seeds

semifreddi, (half-cold) desserts frozen or refrigerated before service

semigreggio integrale, semi-whole wheat rice

semolino, flour

semplice, plain
senape, mustard
senza, without
seppia (e), cuttlefish/squid
seppioline, small cuttlefish/squid
serpentone, pastry stuffed w/chopped figs, apples & nuts
servizio, service/service charge
servizio compreso, service included
servizio incluso, service included
servizio non compreso, service not included
servizio non incluso, service not included
sesamo, sesame
sete, thirsty
sevàdas, Sardinian deep-fried pastries
sfilatino, bread loaf
sfogie, Venetian word for sole
sfoglia/sfogliatella/sfogliatelli, flaky-crusted shell-shaped
    pastry filled w/sweetened *ricotta* cheese
sfogliata, flaky pastry
sfogliata di crema, cream puff
sformato, similar to a souffle
sfratti, sweet walnut rolls (a Christmas dessert)
sgavecio, pickled fish
sgombro (i), mackerel
sidro, cider
sigarette, cigarettes
silvano, chocolate tart
Silvestro, herb & mint liqueur
smacafam, *polenta* dish w/*asiago*
    cheese & sausage
Soave, slightly dry white wine from Veneto
sodo/sode, hard boiled
soffritto, sautéed/stock (the base for soup or the sauce for
    pasta) often made w/pigs' organs. Can also refer to slightly
    fried or browned onions, carrots & celery, a base for many
    dishes
sogliola, sole
sogliola all'Arlecchino, sole served w/a cream sauce
sogliola alla mugnaia, sole sautéed w/lemon, butter & parsley
sogliola margherita, sole covered w/hollandaise sauce
soia, soy
sopa, soup

Smacafam means hunger killer

Sogliola SO-LEE-OH-LA

sopa cauda, soup w/bread & roast pigeon
soppressa, sausage
soppressata, sausage/sausage made from pig's head
sorbetto, sherbet/sorbet
sorbetto al calvados, sherbet flavored w/apple brandy
sorrentina, often refers to a tomato, basil & mozzarella sauce
sottaceti, pickles
sottaceto, pickled
sottoaceti, pickled vegetables/pickles
sottofiletto, beef or veal loin
sott'olio, in olive oil
sottonoce, top round of veal
spaccatina, bread loaf
spaghetti, spaghetti (long, thin pasta)
spaghetti aglio e olio, spaghetti w/olive oil & garlic
spaghetti alla bolognese, spaghetti w/meat sauce
spaghetti alla carbonara, spaghetti w/cream, bacon, cheese & egg
spaghetti alla checca, spaghetti w/raw tomatoes, basil & garlic
spaghetti alla gricia, spaghetti w/onions, bacon, pepper & grated cheese
spaghetti all'amatriciana, w/tomato sauce, cheese & garlic
spaghetti alle vongole, spaghetti w/clam sauce
spaghetti al ragù, pasta w/meat & tomato sauce
spaghettini, thin spaghetti
spaghetti pomodoro e basilico, spaghetti w/tomatoes & basil
spalla, shoulder
spanocci, very large prawns
sparaci, asparagus in Venice
sparnocci, type of shrimp
specialità della casa, specialty of the house
specialità di questa regione, specialty of the region
specialità di questo ristorante, specialty of the restaurant
specialità locali, local specialties
specialità regionali, regional specialties/local dishes
speck, cured ham found in the Trentino-Alto Adige region
spelt, a hard wheat
speziato, spicy
spezie, spice
spezzatino, meat or poultry stew/little pieces
spezzato, a stew
spicchio (d'aglio), clove (of garlic)

Sottoaceti means under vinegar

spiedini alla corsara flambe, grilled meat served "flaming"
spiedini di mare, pieces of grilled fish on a skewer
spiedino (i), any dish roasted on a skewer
spiedo, allo, on a spit
spiga di grano, ear of corn
spigola, sea bass/grouper
spinaci, spinach
spiza di grano, ear of corn
spremuta, fresh fruit drink
spugnola, morel mushroom
spuma, mousse
spumante, sparkling wine
spumone (i), ice cream w/candied fruit, nuts & whipped cream
spumoni al croccante, *spumoni* topped w/toasted,
    caramelized almonds
spuntatura, breast of...
spuntino, snack
stagionato (a), well aged
stagione (i), season (in season)
starna, a type of partridge
stecca di, bar of
stecchi fritti, fried kebabs
stecchino, toothpick/skewer
stellette/stelline, star-shaped pasta
stinchetti, marzipan cakes (in the shape of human bones)
stinco, braised veal or pork shank. The most common version
    of this dish is ***stinco di maiale al forno***, a whole pork shank
    oven-roasted w/wine, garlic & rosemary
stoccafisso, dried cod
storione, sturgeon
stracchino, a soft, creamy white cheese
stracciate, scrambled eggs
stracciatella, egg-drop soup. This can also
    refer to chocolate-chip ice cream
stracotto, beef stew w/pork sausage/
    pot roast
strangolapreti, see *strozzapreti*
strangozze, see *stringozzi*
strapazzate, scrambled
strascinati, shell-shaped pasta
stravecchio, *parmesan* cheese aged at least three years
Strega, a strong herb liqueur

Stinco actually means shin bone.

89

strigghie, red mullet in Sicily

stringozzi, a homemade pasta from Umbria

strisce, ribbon noodles

strozzapreti, dumplings or *gnocchi* w/meat sauce.

Strozzapreti means Priest stranglers. A gluttonous priest supposedly choked to death on one.

strudel, this famous pastry roll can be found in Trentino-Alto Adige

strutto, lard

stufatino, pot roast or stew

stufato, braised/stewed/stew

stuzzicadenti, toothpicks

stuzzichino (i), appetizer

succhi di frutta, sweetened fruit juice

succo, juice

succo di frutta, fruit juice

succu tunnu, dumpling soup

Succu tunnu. Never had it but love the name.

sufflé, soufflé

sugna, lard

sugna piccante, a spicy sauce made from pork fat (added to dishes in Basilicata)

sugo, sauce/gravy/juice

sugo, al, w/tomato sauce

suino, pork

suppli/suppli di riso, breaded & deep-fried rice balls usually filled w/ham & cheese

suprema di pollo in gelatina, chicken breast in aspic

suro, mackerel

susina (e), plum

tacchino, turkey

tacchino TA-KEE-NO

tagliata di manzo, grilled beef

tagliatelle, short ribbon noodles

taglierini, thin noodles

taglierini alla chitarra, a pasta dish featuring a sheet of pasta cut w/a cutter called a *"chitarra"* or guitar

tagliolini, very narrow, thin flat noodles

tajarin, egg noodles found in Piedmont & Valle d'Aosta

taleggio, cheese w/a mild, buttery flavor

taralli, biscuits made in the shape of a ring

tartara, alla, raw w/lemon sauce

tartaruga, turtle

tartina (e), open-faced sandwich/tart.
   Tartine are often appetizers
tartufi di cioccolato, chocolate "truffles"
   (chocolate-coated ice cream)
tartufi di mare, small clams/cockles
tartufo (i), truffle (funghi that grows around tree trunks)
tartufo di gelato, ice cream w/chocolate sauce
tartufo nero, black truffle from Tuscany
tasse, taxes. Menus will often indicate if *tasse e servizio* (taxes
   & service) are included
tavola (o), table
tavola calda, snack bar/fast food
tavoletta di cioccolata, chocolate bar
tazza, cup
tè, tea
tè cinese, Chinese tea
tè d'India, Indian tea
tè freddo, iced tea
tegamaccio, lake-fish stew from Umbria
tegame/tegamino, al, sautéed
teglia, alla, pan-fried
teglia di pesce spada, marinated swordfish dish
tellina (e), clam
teneroni, veal chops
terrina, tureen
testa, head. *Testa di vitello* is calf's head
testina, head
testuggine, turtle
tiedde, fish casserole from Apulia
tiella, any dish with baked layers of ingredients
tiella di agnello, roasted lamb dish
tiella di riso e cozze, mussels, rice & potato dish found in
   Apulia
tigelle, flat bread
timbale/timballo, meat & vegetable casserole w/layers of pasta
timo, thyme
tinca (tinche), tench (seafood)
tiramisù, spongecake soaked in
   espresso & brandy w/cream &
   chocolate. *Marsala* can also
   be used in this
   delicious dessert

tirolese, alla, usually means
   w/fried onion rings
tisana, herbal tea
tisana al cinorrode, rose-hip tea
tisana al tiglio, lime tea
tisana camomilla, camomile tea
tocco di funghi, mushroom sauce
toc de purcit, pork stew w/white wine from
   Friuli-Venezia Giulia
toma, sharp cheese
tomini, fresh cheese from Piedmont
tonarelli/tonarrelli/tonnarelli, thin string pasta
tondino, bread loaf
tonica, tonic water
tonnato, in a tuna sauce. Can also refer to a cold veal dish
tonnetto, small tuna
tonno, tuna
topinambur, artichoke
   (Jerusalem artichoke)
tordo (i), thrush (a bird)
torlo, yolk
torrone, nougat
torta (e), tort/cake/pie

Torrone is immensely popular in Italy.

torta al pesto, spinach & cheese pie/flat
   bread cooked over hot stones in Umbria
   & filled w/cheese, meat or greens
torta di frutta, fruit tart
torta di gelato, ice-cream cake *— yes please.*
torta di mele, apple tart
torta di tagliatelle, egg-noodle cake
torta di verdure, sweet vegetable pie
   (similar to American pumpkin pie)
torta gianduia, chocolate & nut cake
torta meringa, large meringue pie filled w/fruit & topped
   w/whipped cream
torta millefoglie, napoleon (layers of pastry filled w/ice cream
   or whipped cream & topped w/frosting)
torta Pasqualina, Easter puff-pastry cake
torta rustica, cornmeal-cake dessert
torta sbrisolona, flour, cornmeal & almond cake
   (crumble cake)
torta tarantina, potato pie

torta turchesca, rice-pudding tart from Venice

torta zuccotto, liquor-soaked sponge cake filled w/ice cream or whipped cream, chocolate & candied fruits

tortelli di zucca, pasta stuffed w/pumpkin

tortellini, filled pasta rings

tortello (i), small doughnut/fritter

tortellone (i), a larger *tortellini* pasta

tortiera, cake/pie

tortiglione, almond cakes

tortiglioni, tube-shaped pasta (larger than *cannelloni*)

tortina di marmellata, jam tart

tortini di riso, rice cakes

tortino, tart/cheese & vegetable tart similar to quiche

tortino di carciofi, dish of fried artichokes & eggs

toscana, alla, w/tomatoes & herbs

tostato (a), toasted

totano (i), squid

tournedos, small tenderloin steaks

tovaglia, table cloth

tovagliolo, napkin

Tovagliolo
TOV - A - LEE - OH - LO

tozzetti, hazelnut & almond biscuits (flavored w/anise)

tracina dragone, a fish named "dragon" after its dangerous spines

tramezzino, small sandwich

trancia/trancio, piece/slice

trattaliu, cooked lamb intestines. A specialty in Sardinia

trenette, long, flat, thin ribbon noodles

trifolati, sliced mushrooms cooked in butter, garlic & oil

trifolato, w/truffles

triglia (e), red mullet

triglia alla Livornese, red mullet cooked w/tomatoes, garlic & parsley

trigoli, water chestnuts

trippa (e), tripe

trippa alla fiorentina, braised tripe & minced beef w/tomato sauce & cheese

trippa alla milanese, tripe w/onions, carrots, tomatoes, beans & leeks

trippa alla romana, tripe in a tomato & vegetable sauce

You can put all the "ALLA's" you want on trippa and it's still TRIPE.

93

tritato (a), ground (as in ground beef)

trofie, pasta similar to *gnocchi*

trombetta da morto, a type of mushroom

trota (e), trout

trota alle mandorle, stuffed-trout dish

trota di ruscello, river trout

trota iridea, rainbow trout

trota salmonata, salmon trout

trota spaccata, trout split in two, dipped in batter & deep-fried

trotella, trout

tuaca, a mixture of brandy, citrus fruits & herbs

tubetti, *macaroni*

tubi, refers to all tubular pasta

tuorlo, yolk

tutto compreso, all included

ua, grapes in Venice

ubriaco, cooked in red wine

uccelletti/uccelli, small birds (of
    all kinds) usually spit-roasted

uccelletto, all', w/tomato sauce & sage. *Piselli all' uccelletto*
    are peas cooked in tomato sauce w/sage

uccelli scappati, pork, pork sausage &/or small-bird kebabs

ueta, raisin in Venice

uliva, olive

umido, in, stewed

uopa, sea bream

uova, eggs

uova affogate, poached eggs

uova affogate nel vino, eggs poached in wine

uova à la coque, soft-boiled eggs

uova albume, egg whites

uova al burro, eggs fried in butter

uova al guscio, soft-boiled eggs

uova alla campagnola, eggs w/diced vegetables & cheese

uova alla coque, boiled eggs

uova alla fiorentina, fried eggs served on spinach

uova all'americana, fried eggs (usually served w/bacon)

uova alla russa, similar to deviled eggs

uova all'occhio di bue, fried eggs

uova al tegame con formaggio, fried eggs w/cheese

uova barrotte, soft-boiled eggs

uova bollite, soft-boiled eggs

uova frittata/uova fritte, fried omelette
uova frittata al pomodoro, tomato omelette
uova frittata al prosciutto, ham omelette
uova in camicia, poached eggs
uova molli/uova mollette, soft-boiled eggs
uova ripiene, stuffed eggs
uova semplice, plain omelette
uova sode agli spinaci, eggs florentine
uova tonnate, hard-boiled eggs in tuna sauce
uovo (a), egg
uovo fritto (uova fritte), fried egg
uovo sodo (uova sode), hard-boiled egg
uovo strapazzatto (uova strapazzate), scrambled egg
uva, grapes
uva bianca, green grapes
uva nera, black grapes
uva passa/uva passita, raisins
uva secca, raisin
uva spina, gooseberry
uvetta, white raisins
vaniglia, vanilla
valdostana, alla, usually means served w/ham & cheese
    (means "Valle d'Aosta style")
valigetta, roasted veal breast
Valpolicella, light (slightly bitter) red wine from Veneto
vapore, a, steamed
vario/vari, assorted
Vecchia Romagna, wine-distilled brandy
vegetable, vegetable
vegetariano (a), vegetarian
velluta, creamy soup
veneziana, alla, w/onions, white wine & sometimes mint
ventaglio, scallop
ventresca, white-meat tuna. Can also mean a boiled pork dish
verde, green/green pasta (w/a spinach base)
verde in pinzimonio, vegetable dip
Verdicchio, a dry white wine from Le Marche
verdura (e), green vegetable
verdura trovata, sautéed wild greens w/potatoes
verdure cotte, cooked vegetables
vermicelli, thin, long spaghetti noodles
vermut, vermouth

verza, cabbage

verzelata, grey mullet

vincigrassi/vincisgrassi, baked lasagna dish. Named after an
Austrian prince, this dish is a specialty in the region of Le
Marche where it's usually served w/chicken-giblet sauce

vincotto, a spread made from grapes

vinello, light wine

vino (i), wine

vino amabile, sweet wine

vino asciutto, very dry wine

vino bianco, white wine

vino brut, very dry wine

vino corposo, full-bodied wine

vino da pasto, table wine

vino da tavola, table wine
(the lowest-quality wine made
from any combination of grapes)

amabile also means loveable which pretty much refers to all wine as far as we're concerned.

vino del paese, local wine

vino dolce, sweet wine

vino frizzante, sparkling wine

vino leggero, light wine

vino nostrano, local wine

vino novello, new wine

vino rosatello, rosé wine

vino rosato, rosé wine

vino rosé, rosé (blush) wine

vino roseo, rosé wine

vino rosso, red wine

vino da tavola is low quality wine but not necessarily bad.

Vin Santo/Vinsanto, dessert wine from Tuscany & Trentino

vino secco, dry wine

vino semi secco, semi-sweet wine

vino spumante, sparkling wine

vino tipico, local wine

violino, cured leg of goat

visciola, wild cherry

vitellini, very young veal

vitello, veal

vitello all'uccelletto, diced veal & sage simmered in wine

vitello tonnato, cold veal w/tuna sauce

vodka, vodka

vol-au-vents, filled pastry shells

vongola (e), small clam

You weren't really looking this up were you?

vongole, alle, in a clam sauce

vongole oreganate, clams baked or broiled w/oregano

vongole veraci, small clams boiled in vinegar,
hot pepper & garlic

whisky, whiskey

wurstel, hot dogs (similar to smoked hot dogs)

yogurt/yoghurt, yogurt

yogurt magro, low-calorie yogurt. *Yogurt intero* is not low-fat

zabaglione/zabaione, custard dessert flavored w/Marsala

zafferano, saffron

zalettini, shortbread cookies from Venice   *I'll pass.*

zampa (e), pig's (or beef) feet

zampetto, pork leg

zampone, large pig's foot scraped clean of its insides & then
stuffed w/spicy sausage

zampone di maiale, stuffed pigs' feet

zelten, dried fruit & nut cake from Trentino-Alto Adige

zenzero, ginger

zèppola, doughnut/fritter   *— Si, grazie!*

zesti, orange or lemon peel (can also be candied)

ziba, fragrant herb from Sardinia

zimini, in, cooked w/vegetables. *In zimino* can refer to spinach
or Swiss chard stewed w/cod or squid & tomatoes

zimino, Sardinian fish stew

zingara, alla, "Gypsy style." Each chef has his or her own
version of this sauce of many ingredients

zite (i), narrow, hollow-tube pasta

zucca, pumpkin or squash

zucca ovifera, squash

zucchero, sugar

zucchero a velo, powdered sugar

zucchero a zollette, lump sugar

zucchero greggio, brown sugar

zucchero grezzo, brown sugar   *Zuchine*

zucchero in pezzi, lump sugar   *ZOO·KEEN·E*

zucchero in polvere, powdered sugar

zucchine al burro versato, zucchini w/black-butter sauce

zucchine farcite, zucchini filled cheese, ham & mushrooms

zucchine fritte, deep-fried strips of zucchini

zucchine scapecce, pieces of zucchini fried in oil w/garlic

zucchine trifolate, sliced zucchini in butter, parsley & garlic

zucchino (i), zucchini

zucchina (e), zucchini
zuccotto, ice cream-filled cake
zuchette, zucchini
zuppa, soup
zuppa alla coltivatore, vegetable soup with diced bacon
zuppa alla pavese, soup w/croutons, grated cheese & poached egg
zuppa di arzilla, soup made w/ray fish & broccoli
zuppa di cereali, bean, vegetable & grain stew
zuppa di cipolle alla Francese, french onion soup
zuppa di cozze, mussel soup
zuppa di datteri, fish-soup specialty of Liguria
zuppa di fagioli, bean soup
zuppa di farro, soup made with *farro* (a wheat similar to spelt)
zuppa di frutti di mare, seafood soup
zuppa di lenticchie, lentil soup
zuppa di pesce, fish stew
zuppa di pollo, chicken soup
zuppa di telline, soup w/tiny clams
zuppa di verdura, vegetable soup
zuppa di vongole, clam soup w/white wine
zuppa d'orzo, barley & potato soup
zuppa fredda, cold soup
zuppa inglese, not a soup at all. Spongecake soaked in liquor w/cream filling & whipped cream
zuppa pavese, clear soup w/a poached egg
zuppa valdostana, cabbage soup from the Val d'Aosta region
zuppa di zucca, soup made from small squash or pumpkin

Zuppa di farro... Love it.

Buon Appetito!

Phone numbers, days closed and hours of operation often change, so it's advisable to check ahead. Restaurants in tourist areas may have different hours and days of operation during low season. Reservations are recommended for all restaurants unless noted.

Prices are for main courses and without wine. Lunch, even at the most expensive restaurants listed below, always has a lower fixed price. Credit cards are accepted unless noted otherwise.

Inexpensive: under 10 euros
Moderate: 11 – 20 euros
Expensive: 21 – 30 euros
Very Expensive: over 30 euros

Dialing the telephone in Italy
The country code for Italy is 39.
The area code for Venice is 041.
Calling Venice from the US and
    Canada: 011+39+041+the local
    number.
Calling Venice from the UK:
    00+39+041+the local number.
Calling within Italy (for example
    from Florence to Venice): 041+
    the local number.
Calling from Italy to the US and
    Canada: 00+1+area code+the
    local number
Calling from Italy to the UK:
    00+44+area code+local number.
Telephone numbers in Venice that
    do not begin with 041 are cell
    phone numbers.

We think, hope and pray that our restaurant list is current & correct, but remember... things change. Call first or do a "walk-by" in the afternoon. Stop in, make a reservation — they'll love you for it.

Antico Giardinetto

Friendly, informal, family-run *osteria*. Try the *filetto di manzo al 3 pepi* (filet of beef with pepper sauce) or *costolette d'agnello toscano scottadito* (Tuscan roasted lamb chops). There are many seafood options on the menu, including *sauté di cozze e vongole* (sautéed mussels and clams). Decent house red wine, too. *Info*: 2253 Santa Croce, Calle dei Morti (near Campo San Cassiano). Rialto vaporetto. Tel. 041/722882. www.anticogiardinetto.it. Closed Mon and part of Jan. No lunch. Moderate – Expensive. Map B #1.

Il Refolo

This pizzeria/restaurant is on a picturesque square overlooking the church of San Giacomo dell'Orio. Customers dock their boats along the patio for take-out. Try the pizza topped with a local specialty, *castraure* (the first floral shoot of the artichoke). One pizza on the menu features roasted figs and *prosciutto*. *Info*: 1459 Santa Croce. Campiello del Piovan (Campo San Giacomo dell'Orio). Riva di Biasio or San Stae vaporetto. Tel. 041/5240016. Closed Mon and Dec-Mar. Moderate. Map B #2.

La Bottiglia

Dining in Venice can be expensive, but that doesn't mean that you have to spend a lot of money to have good food. This simple eatery is near the Basilica di Santa Maria Gloriosa dei Frari. Choose your meat and cheese and create a *panini* (sandwich) on *focaccia* (flat oven-baked bread similar to pizza dough). There's no indoor seating, but a few tables outside are near the canal. Good local wine and beer. *Info*: 2537 San Polo. Campo San Stin. San Toma vaporetto. Tel. 3355930910. Open daily. Inexpensive. Map: B #3.

Al Bacco Felice

Just a ten-minute walk from Piazzale Roma, this neighborhood restaurant and pizzeria is popular with both locals and tourists. Nothing fancy here. Pizza, pasta and traditional Italian dishes like *pasta arrabbiata* (pasta with a spicy tomato and herb sauce). Complimentary Venetian cookies are served at the end of your meal. *Info*: 197/e Santa Croce on Corte dei Amai. Piazzale Roma vaporetto. Tel. 041/5287794. Open daily. Moderate. Map B #4.

Da Ivo

Beautiful restaurant serving Venetian (and Tuscan) specialties. Try the delicious *bistecca alla Fiorentina* (T-bone steak).
We came here before celebrities like George Clooney came
here. So, he's just copying us. *Info*: 1809 San Marco. Calle dei
Fuseri (near Campo S. Luca). Tel. 041/5285004.
www.ristorantedaivo.it. Closed Sun and Jan. San Marco
vaporetto. Expensive – Very Expensive. Map D #5.

Enoteca al Volto

This wine bar has wooden tables and chairs, wine labels as
wallpaper, an impressive wine list, and simple Venetian fare.
Try the *ravioloni di asparagi con capesante e fiori di zucca*
(asparagus ravioli with scallops and zucchini flowers). A great
deal. *Info*: 4081 San Marco. Calle Cavalli (near Campo Chiesa
and Campo San Luca). Rialto vaporetto. Tel. 041/5228945.
www.enotecaalvolto.com. Open daily. Moderate. Map D #6.

Da Mamo

Pasta, pizza, and large salads at this cozy and casual *trattoria*.
Good value. Try the *pizza diavola* with tomato, mozzarella,
and spicy salami. Although it's a bit corny, they have a *pizza
zodiaco* menu featuring a pizza named after the twelve signs of
the zodiac. *Pizza toro* (Taurus) is topped with tomato, mozzarella, sausage, brie, and pepperoni. *Info*: 5251 San Marco. Calle
Stagneri (near Campo San Bartolomio). Rialto vaporetto. Tel.
041/5236583. www.damamo.it. Open daily. Moderate.
Map D #7.

Vino Vino

Popular wine bar and restaurant (near the Teatro La Fenice)
serving typical Venetian cuisine and offering 200 Italian and
imported wines by the bottle or glass. Try the local specialty,
sarde in saor (sardines in a sweet-and-sour sauce). *Info*: 2007A
San Marco. Ponte delle Veste (between La Fenice and via XXII
Marzo). Tel. 041/2417688. www.vinovinowine.com. Open
daily. Vaporetto: S. Maria del Giglio. Moderate. Map D #8.

Dal Moro's - Fresh Pasta To Go

This unassuming and hard to find take-out place is hugely popular. Pasta is made fresh on the premises, and you can order any number of sauces. The *arrabbiata* (spicy tomato and herb sauce) is particularly good. A great way to save money in Venice, where dining can be quite expensive. Each serving costs around €7. Despite the crowds, the servers are very friendly. *Info*: 5324 Castello. Calle de la Casseleria (near the church of Santa Maria Formoso). Rialto or San Marcovaporetto. Tel. 041/4762876. www.dalmorosfreshpastato-go.com. Open daily. No credit cards. Closed Sun. Inexpensive. Map D #9.

Al Mascaron

You might have to sit next to strangers (mostly tourists) at long tables in this unpretentious restaurant/bar. The food is straightforward Venetian. Try the deep-fried *calamari*. The specialty here is *spaghetti allo scoglio* (spaghetti with lobster, shrimp, and scallops). *Info*: 5225 Castello. Calle Lunga Santa Maria Formosa (near the Campo Santa Maria Formosa). Rialto vaporetto. Tel. 041/5225995. www.osteriamascaron.it. Closed Sun and Jan. No credit cards. Moderate. Map D #10.

Oliva Nera

Expect a warm welcome at this small, charming *osteria*. Try the *ossobuco* (braised veal shank), *baccala* (salt cod), or dishes served with *nero di seppia* (black squid ink). You might even leave with a complimentary bottle of the house olive oil. *Info*: 3417/3447 Castello. From Riva degli Schiavoni (on the waterfront), turn onto Calle della Pietà, left on Calle Bosello to Salizada dei Greci. San Zaccaria vaporetto. Tel. 041/5222170. www.olivanera.com. Closed Wed. Moderate – Expensive. Map E #11.

Al Covo

Fresh Venetian specialties (especially seafood) at this small *osteria*. Try the *fritto misto* (mixed deep-fried fish). *Info*: 3968 Castello. Campiello della Pescaria (off of Riva degli Schiavoni). Arsenale vaporetto. Tel. 041/5223812. www.ris-torantealcovo.com. Closed Wed and Thu. Expensive. Map E #12.

Malibran

Intimate restaurant, complete with Venetian-glass chandeliers, near the Rialto Bridge. Italian dishes and homemade pizza. The interesting *pizza della casa* has tomatoes, mozzarella, ham, mushrooms, salami, artichokes, and an egg on top. Pasta dishes include *tortellini panna, prosciutto, e funghi* (tortellini pasta with cream, ham, and mushrooms). *Info*: 5864 Cannaregio. Off of Salizzada San Giovanni Grisostomo and overlooking the Teatro Malibran. Rialto vaporetto. Tel. 041/5228028. www.hotelmalibran.com. Open daily. Moderate. Map D #13.

Vini da Gigio

Wine bar and *osteria* serving Venetian specialties and home-made pasta. Delicious *gnocchi*. There are two seatings on Sat and Sun (7pm and 9pm). *Info*: 3628A Cannaregio. Fondamenta San Felice (just off the Strada Nuova). Cá d'Oro vaporetto. Tel. 041/5285140. www.vinidagigio.com. Closed Mon, Tue, part of Jan and part of Aug. Moderate – Expensive. Map A #14.

Osteria al Cicheto

This small *bacaro* (small, local bar) is near the Santa Lucia train station. If you just want to sample *cicheti*, head to the bar. You'll have a choice of at least ten wines by the glass, most from the Veneto region. If you want to dine, make reservations as there are only a few tables. You'll dine on Venetian specialties such as *fegato alla veneziana con i fichi* (liver with figs) and *pasta e fagioli all veneta* (Venetian pasta and beans). You'll have an interesting experience! *Info*: 367/A Cannaregio. Calle della Misericordia. Ferrovia vaporetto. Tel. 041/716037. Closed Sat (lunch) and Sun. www.osteria-al-cicheto.it. Moderate. Map A #15.

Ai Gondolieri

Not for seafood lovers. This restaurant serves meat dishes like *ossobuco di vitello* (braised veal shank). Try the creamy *risotto con funghi porcini* (risotto with porcini mushrooms). Delicious *fiori di zucca* (zucchini flowers filled w/cheese, then battered and fried). *Info*: 366 Dorsoduro. Calle S. Domenico Dorsoduro. Fondamenta dell'Ospedaleto (near the Guggenheim Museum at Fondamenta Venier dai Leoni). Accademia vaporetto. Tel.

041/5286396. www.aigondolieri.it. Open daily. Moderate –
Expensive. Map C #16.

La Bitta
In a small storefront, this family-owned restaurant and wine
bar focuses on meat dishes (often accompanied by grilled
vegetables). The *porchetta* (roast suckling pig stuffed with
herbs), served with a horseradish sauce, is delicious. The menu
also features dishes served with *peverada* (a spicy sauce with
chicken livers and anchovies). Desserts include an excellent
panna cotta (rich cream custard). Wine comes in a bottle, but
you only pay for what you've consumed. End your meal with
grappa. *Info*: 2753A Dorsoduro. Calle Lunga San Barnaba
(off of Campo San Barnaba). Ca' Rezzonico vaporetto. Tel.
041/5230531. Closed Sun and part of Jul. No lunch. No credit
cards. Moderate. Map C #17.

Cantine del Vino gìa Schiavi
You'll find a decent selection of Italian wine by the bottle at
this wine shop. Head to the bar (there's no seating here) where
you can sample *cicchetti* for around €2. Try the interesting
specialty *tartare di tonno*, tuna dusted with unsweetened cocoa
powder. There's a large selection of wine by the glass, most
from the Veneto region, starting at €2. If you ask for a *fuori*,
you'll be served your wine in a plastic cup so that you can take
it outside. *Info*: 992 Dorsoduro.(near the Accademia Museum
on the San Trovaso canal). Zattere or Accademia vaporetto. Tel.
041/5230034. Open 8:30am-10:30pm. Closed Sun.
www.cantinaschiavi.com. Inexpensive. Map: C #18.

Estro
This wine bar and restaurant is decorated with wood furnish-
ings and Murano glass. The vast wine list features more than
600 wines mostly from Italy and France. If you dine here, start
with the house specialty *baccala mantecato* (creamed cod) and
don't miss the rich lasagna with veal ragout and parmigiano
reggiano. *Info*: 3778 Dorsoduro. Calle San Pantalon. San Toma
vaporetto. www.estrovenezia.com. Tel. 041/4764914. Closed
Tue. Map B #19.

Rialto Market
(Rialto vaporetto)
Produce Market: Mon-Sat 7:30am-1pm
Fish Market at Campo de la Pescheria: Tue-Sat 7;30am-1pm.
.

Garibaldi Market on via Giuseppe Garibaldi
(Arsenale vaporetto)
Mon-Fri 8am-noon.

Caffè Florian

Piazza San Marco (St. Mark's Square) is home to this elegant and expensive café. It has been in business since 1720, and it's worth the splurge to sit and listen to the orchestra in one of the world's loveliest squares. In fact, you'll pay more when the orchestra performs. When the weather isn't great, you can sit inside surrounded by mirrors, statues, and frescoes. Expect to pay at least €20 for a Bellini (*prosecco* and peach nectar). *Info*: 56 Piazza San Marco. San Marco vaporetto. Tel. 041/5205641. Closed Wed in winter. Open daily 9am-midnight. www.caffe-florian.com. Map D #20.

Al Prosecco

You can't come to Italy and not sample *prosecco*. This sparkling white wine will tickle your tongue and quench your thirst, especially on a warm Venetian night. Great terrace and simple *cichetti* (the Venetian version of Spanish *tapas*). A glass of *prosecco* begins at €4 and goes up from there. *Info*: 1503 Santa Croce. Campo San Giacomo de l'Orio. San Stae vaporetto. Tel. 041/5240222. Closed Sun, Aug, and Jan. www.alprosecco.com. Map B #21.

Harry's Bar

Travelers continue to flock to Harry's Bar just west of St. Mark's Square. Although dinner is extremely expensive (and many complain not worth the cost), most come to have a martini or delicious Bellini (sparkling *prosecco* and peach nectar) at the bar. The drink will cost you around €20, so drink it slowly! If it was good enough for Ernest Hemingway and Truman Capote, it should be good enough for you. *Info*: 1323 Calle Vallaresso. San Marco vaporetto. Tel 041/5285777. Open daily. www.cipriani.com. Map D #22.

Cicheti, the Venetian version of *tapas*, are served at *bacari* (small, local bars) with glasses of wine. Starting at as little as €1, you'll pay a fraction of the cost that you would at a café. It's a great way to eat on a budget. Here are a few places to try *cicheti*. (All are near the Rialto vaporetto)

Cantina do Mori
429 San Polo. Calle do Mori and Calle Miani (on the San Polo side of Rialto Bridge, walk to end of the market stalls, turn left and then immediately right). Tel. 041/5225401. Closed Sun. Try the *melanzane alla parmigiana* (eggplant parmesan). Map F #1.

Bancogiro
122 San Polo. Campo San Giacometto (west end of Rialto Bridge along the Grand Canal). Tel. 041/5232061. Closed Mon. www.osteriabancogiro.it. Try the *selezione di formaggi* (cheese plate). Map F #2.

Al Mercà
213 San Polo. Campo Cesare Battisti. On a picturesque square in Rialto Markets area (off of Fondamenta Riva Olio). Tel. 347/1002583. www.osteriaalmerca.it. Try the *robiola* (soft, mild, and slightly sweet cheese). Map F #3.

Cantina Do Spade
859 San Polo. 19 Calle Do Spade, On a narrow alleyway near Campo Beccarie. Tel. 041/5210583. www.cantinadospade.com. No lunch Tue. Try the *calamari fritti* (fried squid). Map F #4.

All'Arco
436 San Polo. Calle Arco. Calle de l'Ochialer. Tel. 041/5205666. Closed Sun. Try the *acciughe* (anchovies). Map F #5.

These are some dining specialties found in Venice and the Veneto region. Certain food items are called by different names in Venice than the rest of Italy. We've included them, too.

anguilla alla veneziana, eel braised w/tuna & lemon sauce
bellini, *prosecco* & peach juice. Try one at Harry's Bar
bovoletti/bovoloni, small snails
canoce, Venetian word for *cannocchie* which is neither a
   shrimp nor a lobster but something in between
cape sante, scallops
carpaccio, thinly sliced raw beef w/sauce. Named by the owner
   of Harry's Bar in Venice after a famous Venetian painter
cicchetti/cicheti, snacks served in Venice. Similar to *tapas*
fegà, liver
folpetto, baby octopus
granceola/ granseola, spider crab
lissa, pompano (fish)
masenette, small soft-shelled crabs
nervetti, calf's foot dish (tendons of calves' feet)
ombra, glass of wine. This word is usually used at a bar & not
   at a restaurant
pasticcio, the Venetian word for baked lasagne
pesce in saor, fish in a sauce of onion, raisin, pine nut &
   vinegar. A specialty in Veneto
pinza, yellow flour, pine nut & raisin cake from Veneto
prosecco, sparkling white wine from Veneto
risi e bisi, creamy rice w/green peas.
   Bisi is the Venetian word for peas
risotto alla Veneta, rice w/mussels
schila, shrimp
sfogie, Venetian word for sole
Soave, slightly dry white wine from Veneto
sparaci, asparagus
torta turchesca, rice-pudding tart
ua, grapes
Valpolicella, light (slightly bitter) red wine from Veneto
veneziana, alla, usually means w/onions, white wine &
   sometimes mint
ueta, raisin
zalettini, shortbread cookies

Venice

1. Basilica di San Marco
   (St. Mark's Basilica)
2. Canal Grande
   (Grand Canal)
3. Ca' d'Oro
   (House of Gold)
4. Ca' Rezzonico
5. Collezione Peggy Guggenheim
   (Peggy Guggenheim Collection)
6. Gallerie dell'Accademia
   (Academy Gallery)
7. Ghetto (Jewish Ghetto)
8. Giudecca
9. Madonna dell'Orto
10. Museo Civico Correr
    (Correr Civic Museum)
11. Museo Storico Navale
    (Naval Museum)
12. Palazzo Ducale
    (Doge's Palace)
13. Piazza San Marco
    (St. Mark's Square)
14. Ponte di Rialto
    (Rialto Bridge)
15. San Giorgio Maggiore
16. Santa Maria della Salute
17. Santa Maria Gloriosa dei Frari
18. Scuola Grande di San Rocco
19. Teatro La Fenice

Venice Map A

CANNAREGIO

Venice Map C

113

Venice Map D

Venice Map E

Map F

ITALY

Europe Made Easy Travel Guides

Eating & Drinking Guides
Menu Translators and Restaurant Guides

- *Eating & Drinking in Paris*
- *Eating & Drinking in Italy*
- *Eating & Drinking in Spain and Portugal*
- *Eating & Drinking in Latin America*

Europe Made Easy Travel Guides

- *Amsterdam Made Easy*
- *Barcelona Made Easy*
- *Berlin Made Easy*
- *Europe Made Easy*
- *French Riviera Made Easy*
- *Italy Made Easy*
- *Oslo Made Easy*
- *Paris Made Easy*
- *Paris Walks*
- *Provence Made Easy*

For a list of all Europe Made Easy travel guides, and to purchase our books, visit www.eatndrink.com